Breaking Free from Corporate Bondage

Do What You *Really* Want To Do and Control Your Own Future

Michael Dainard

Enterprise · Dearborn

a division of Dearborn Publishing Group, Inc.

While a great deal of care has been taken to provide accurate and current information, the ideas, suggestions, general principles and conclusions presented in this text are subject to local, state and federal laws and regulations, court cases and any revisions of same. The reader is thus urged to consult legal counsel regarding any points of law—this publication should not be used as a substitute for competent legal advice.

Publisher: Kathleen A. Welton
Associate Editor: Karen A. Christensen
Interior Design: Professional Resources & Communications, Inc.
Cover Design: Westdal Design

Published by Enterprise • Dearborn
a division of Dearborn Publishing Group, Inc.

Printed in the United States of America

93 94 95 10 9 8 7 6 5 4 3 2 1

Library of Congress Cataloging-in-Publication Data

Dainard, Michael, 1944–
    Breaking free from corporate bondage : do what you really want to do and control your own future / Michael Dainard.
        p. cm.
    Includes index.
    ISBN 0-79310-575-7
    1. Career changes. 2. New business enterprises. I. Title.
HF5384.D34 1993   92-45058
338'.04'0922—dc20   CIP

For Stefan Michael

Most men would feel insulted if it were proposed to employ them in throwing stones over a wall, and then in throwing them back, merely that they might earn their wages. But many are no more worthily employed now.

Thoreau, *Life Without Principle*

Acknowledgments

I would like to thank the many people who gave so generously of their time to help make *Breaking Free* possible:

Dr. Allan B. Astrow, Aaron Baer, Gail Barker, Pamela Bayne, Walter Bodkin, Cassandra Burwell, Dr. Thomas David, Peter Depetro, Jim Donnelly, Bob Eychner, Dr. Christopher A. Fabian, Hans Frank, Dina Gängl-Ehrenwerth, Dr. Melvin Fishman, Richard Gallagher, Ursel Hatzinger-Winkler, Charles Heisinger, Jr., Dr. David Hendell, Marcia Holdt, Kathrin Hornbanger, Dr. Stuart I. Isler, Barbara Kaplan, Dr. Ernst Kotzman, Andrew Koval, Gretel Lechner, Dr. Michael Liquori, Frederich Lunning, Jim and Madeline Masser, Kevin McCoy, Richard McLoughlin, Dr. Christopher B. Mills, Rick North, Resi Petutschnig, Carl Price, Carl Prut-ting, Karen B. Raugust, Dr. Joseph P. Rocchio, Jr., Ingrid and Jordan Roettele, John Ryan, Dr. Sabitzer, Nathan Sambul, Evelyn Simioli, Eglon Simons, Gerti Svetlik, Ted Walworth, Doris Ward, Karl Wexler, Dr. Hans Winkler, Dr. Hanns M. Winkler, Brigitte Winkler, Ulrike Winkler, Mary Young, David Zema, Art and Roger Zeidman, Dr. Fritz Zitter and the Captains and crews from the ships of the Wörther See and Lendkanal Shipping Company, Klagenfurt, Austria.

Special thanks go to the following who took the time to share their personal experiences:

Pamela Call, M.D., LaVaun S. Eustice, Kathleen M. Giordano, Ambassador Roy M. Huffington, Elmore Leonard, Mark Christopher Lingley, James A. Michener, Scott Powers, David Grant Roth, Wilhelmina Michel-Weng and Bill Young.

And my deep gratitude goes to Mary Rowland, *The New York Times*.

Table of Contents

Part 3: Those Who Did It— How They Did It   91

Foreword

You are perceptive in writing the book on *Breaking Free from Corporate Bondage*, for this is a problem that confronts a huge percentage of men and women in their middle professional years. I have grappled with such confrontations four times.

(1) As a young teacher of English two years out of college, with a secure job in one of America's most prestigious prep schools, I foresaw that I really required some years of study in Europe to round out my own education. I therefore surrendered my job and sped across the ocean to Scotland where I enrolled at a university from which I branched out to all parts of Europe and the Mideast. The remarkable fact about this decision was that all the older men working with me advised against such an irresponsible decision because this was 1931 during the depth of the Depression. They said, "If you leave this job, you may never get another." But I continued on to Europe, and it was one of the best decisions I've ever made.

(2) When I returned from Europe with America still in the grips of the Depression, I was fortunate to find another job immediately. But while working in this job, I discovered that my interests were much broader than the mere teaching of English. At the age of 26, I changed course in mid-ocean and taught myself to be an expert in teaching history. A few years later,

I was a visiting professor of that subject at Harvard University and was on a track that could have led me to a successful career in that exciting field.

(3) While teaching at Harvard, a major publishing company spotted me as having some skill at writing education materials, and I was offered an enticing editorial job in New York. Again, I was on a major fast track and believed that this was to be my career.

(4) In the early stages of World War II, I was drafted into the Army. The day before my induction, however, I enlisted in the Navy. (I decided that I would rather ride to war than walk.) One midnight on a remote airfield on a small island in the South Pacific—after having survived a hairy experience and a near-fatal crash—I decided that the challenges of every occupation I had had at that time had been exhausted. If I survived the War, I was determined to pursue an entirely different career—that of writing books for others to publish and use. Fortunately, my decision was a practical one that has led to considerable satisfaction.

I would suspect that many adults face similar difficult decisions. Not all are free to leave one form of employment and seek another. Some are prohibited by family problems, still others by lack of nerve. Human beings typically experience job change as they strive to build both a satisfactory life and a secure financial base from which to pursue it.

James A. Michener

Preface

I first heard the term *corporate bondage* when I worked at CBS in the mid-1980s. It described the dilemma many of my management friends felt they were in; I felt it myself. We usually referred to it as *golden handcuffs*. As successful 40-something and 50-something executives, we were chained to our companies and our careers. Our titles, salaries, benefits, perks and lifestyles—not to mention our egos—were our handcuffs, the trappings that made it almost impossible to consider a change. We were *successfully unhappy*.

Our unhappiness had nothing to do with CBS per se. It was a symptom shared by many in diverse companies and career fields. My position at CBS allowed access to management people from a vast array of companies across the country and the oceans. Everywhere I went, I heard the same story.

People didn't blurt out their unhappiness. I heard their stories only in confidence after I'd known them for a while and had earned their trust. These were successful people, many at the top of their fields. They weren't whiners. They were, for the most part, extremely competent executives. But late in their careers, they were miserable—and afraid. To look at them, you would never know it. These were people who seemed to have it all.

They were envied, living in rarefied air. How *could they* be unhappy? How *dare they* be unhappy? Families and friends were proud of their accomplishments, which was one of the biggest dilemmas some of them faced.

How can executives break the corporate bondage? Why would they want to? Their salaries support mortgages, several cars, private schools, vacations and luxuries. Other people depend upon them. Wouldn't it be selfish to consider making a change? And besides, at their age they're too old to start new careers. Starting at the beginning again can be as scary as hell.

Don't believe it. Unhappiness and stress can kill you early. You may never live to enjoy retirement. You owe it to yourselves and your families to at least think about your dreams. What do you really want to do? What would make you *really* happy?

These days there's an awful lot to worry about. Many senior-level executives harbor an underlying fear of being fired or having their positions eliminated. The massive mega-mergers and leveraged buyouts of the 1980s junk bond era are still wreaking havoc. What once looked like a secure field is now seriously overcrowded and growing daily. Even the hallowed ground of being a partner in a law firm is no longer secure. Partners are being let go. If the axe falls, where do such people go? These executives are afraid to leave and afraid to stay—immobilized.

People who suddenly find themselves in outplacement should consider whether they want to snap on a new pair of corporate chains right away. Instead, they should stop and think about what they would really like to do. What are their dreams? Now might be the time to do something about making dreams come true. Job loss disasters often turn into golden opportunities.

Those in low-level to mid-level executive positions can feel that they are going nowhere and don't believe they have an alternative. Trapped in a field that pays fairly well and represents security, they are afraid to leave it. They, too, are unhappy.

These are the types of executives I meet in the classes I teach at New York University. Their numbers grow each semester. They are determined to do something to break the corporate bondage.

I broke away from corporate bondage in 1986, leaving the corporate world behind and opening my own small business. I now have time to pursue my greatest love— writing. The early years weren't easy, and I certainly have had my share of criticism from friends and associates for leaving a career that was glamorous and profitable. But I sure am happy. I spend much more time with my family now, and I do what I really love to do every day. It doesn't seem like work even though some weeks I work more hours than I did when I was in the corporate world.

I wrote this book as an outline for a new course I'm teaching at New York University. It is designed to show you a way out, a way to break free from corporate bondage. Escape isn't easy and it won't happen overnight, but the rewards can be tremendous.

Part 1

Your Dream

THE FAR SIDE   By GARY LARSON

Source: The Far Side cartoon by Gary Larson is reprinted by permission of Chronicle Features, San Francisco, California.

Follow Your Dream

It happens all the time. People wake up and realize that they are in jobs they really don't like. Many of them are successful executives, some at the very top of their professions. Why are they dissatisfied? The reasons can be baffling. Some people made early career choices and then discovered that their professions were not what they had expected.

Parental or peer pressure may have pushed them in the beginning, and they may have made a choice to please others. Early career counseling might have pointed out that they had an aptitude and the skills for a particular profession. The job market may have dictated the choice, with opportunity and money being prime factors. For many it's just the simple fact that age and experience uncover different perspectives of the world, different choices and lifestyles that they didn't know existed when they were younger.

Rarely does a person decide on a path early in life and happily stay on it until retirement. Once locked into a career, with many years invested in education and experience, it's extremely hard to break out. People begin to feel chained to the job by the golden handcuffs—the large salary, benefits, expense account, other perks and the feeling of prestige and security. Although they seem to have it all, these are very unhappy people. The saddest part is that most of them give up and never even consider following their dreams.

How To Identify Your Dream

What is your dream? Have you thought about it— *really* thought about it? Are you afraid? Are you locked into a sense of "this is all there is"? Are you stuck in a mindset of inaction, afraid of disappointing your family or friends? Do you fear failure? Do you think you're too old to make a dramatic change? Whatever the reason, you've probably repressed your dream completely, hidden it in a dark dungeon, locked the door and thrown away the key. Break down the door—now. It's pretty frightening, but you can do it.

Let your dream come out into the light of day. Make friends with it again. Embrace it. Seduce it. Don't be ashamed of it; you don't have to tell anyone about it yet. Just concentrate on yourself and your dream. The worst possible thing that can happen is that you might want to lock your dream back up again. I don't think so. This book is about making it happen. It's never too late. James Michener's first book was published when he was 40, and Ray Kroc was in his 50s when he founded McDonald's.

Unlocking My Dream

I was 42 when I dug my dream out of the mausoleum. I hadn't locked it away; I had given it a burial—or thought I had. My dream was still there, barely alive, but I nursed it back to health. It's the best thing that has ever happened to me. I celebrated my 48th birthday while writing this book. I feel like I'm 20 again. I can't believe the energy I have each day even though I work much longer and harder than I ever did in the past.

My dream was to be a writer. I was six years old when my Aunt Vera first let me play with her typewriter. I was 46 when I was finally published—40 long years. At 14 I received my first rejection slip. Humiliated and terrified, I buried it in the backyard and didn't write again for over a year. Even then I wouldn't show my writing to anyone and certainly wouldn't send it out for another rejection. I became a closet writer. Like the secret drinker, I hid my addiction from disapproving eyes. At one point of true paranoia, I rented a large safety deposit box to lock my writing in. Then in 1977, at 33 years old, I was foolish enough to show my writing to someone who ended up telling me all the things that were wrong with it. I don't even remember what the piece was, but I went into a childish rage, collected all my works and burned them. There were thousands of pages, and it took an entire afternoon.

I didn't write again for several years. I became a nervous wreck. I drank, smoked and partied too much—running away. Finally I went into therapy. My psychiatrist and I danced around the issue for several years, digging around in the catacombs of my past until I finally admitted my addiction, my repressed dream—writing.

I had an excellent therapist. He encouraged me to write again. I'll never know if he was lying, but he read my work and told me it was good. Finally I got the nerve to send my writing out. It was very simple, he told me. If you ever want to be a published writer, you must show your work to people. He told me that rejection slips were not to be taken personally; they were not an assault against my inner self. Then he held my hand as I started receiving the rejection slips. I have hundreds today. They don't bother me. I've grown up; I've learned to take the criticism and use it to improve my craft.

During this time of internal conflict, I became fairly successful in the field of advertising and marketing. I made very good money, but I remained extremely unhappy.

I got into advertising almost by accident. I had no idea what I wanted to be when I grew up. Writing was my only love, and I was certain that I couldn't support myself in that field. As a teenager that I held a variety of part-time jobs, but nothing really turned me on.

Where I Came From

My first real job was as an aircraft mechanic for a government contractor in Birmingham, Alabama. Being fairly handy with tools, I advanced quickly and made a good salary. The Cuban crisis was a godsend. I was working 12-hour shifts, 7 days a week, making double and triple time. I thought that was what it was all about, making more money than I had time to spend. Then the contractor announced that the windfall was over. The company had completed the contract early, and I was laid off for three months.

I got a part-time job with the J. C. Penney Company making showcards for merchandise and helping out with displays. The full-time display manager was transferred one week before I was to return to my job as a mechanic, and I was offered his job. Quickly I advanced to become advertising manager for the store, and then for a store group. A local department store sought me out, and I became their advertising manager. In 1969 I was offered a job in New York, and my career path was set.

On My Own

Advertising came easily to me, probably because it did require quite a bit of writing and creativity, and I was able to see my ideas come to life in print and broadcast. For the rest of my corporate career, I never had to look for a job.

The offers came, and I just blindly accepted them, climbing higher in position and salary. I don't think I even tried that hard and never gave it my all. If I had really applied myself, there's no telling how far I could have gone. But deep down I didn't really like it. When I left CBS as director of marketing in 1986, I was determined to break my corporate bondage. It was a dream job, overflowing with the prestige and glamour of television, a good salary, a yearly bonus, benefits, expense account, unlimited travel and, of course, an ego trip.

Over Christmas 1985, my wife, Baerbel, and I were vacationing in the Austrian Alps. Embraced by the tranquility of the snow-covered woods, I wrote a ten-year personal marketing plan. Two months later, I left CBS and opened my own advertising agency in New York. I had no clients, and I was never more scared in my life. There was no more salary, no expense account, no insurance and no office. Even more frightening, we were expecting the planned birth of a child that summer— crazy, right? I'd never been out on my own before. I'd always enjoyed the comfort of a large corporation that provided me with regular paychecks, health and dental care, deducted my taxes and gave me a place to go each day. Now *I* was the corporation. There were no safety nets.

The first year was hard, very hard. I received and turned down more than 20 job offers during that time. I'll admit that a few times I almost weakened and thought about accepting one—especially when my phone wasn't ringing with new business for my agency. I certainly wasn't bored, though. I had a lot of new responsibilities, like renting office space, leasing phone systems and equipment, hiring people, filing corporate paperwork, paying quarterly taxes, choosing health insurance plans. I was spending much more money than was coming in that first year, and I learned the art of cash flow and chasing after business loans. I learned about collecting money from clients while fending off creditor demands.

The beginning of the second year was a little easier, and when I filed my first fiscal corporate tax return, I was surprised that I had survived the first year. I hadn't made any extra money, but I had kept my business going and managed to provide for my family. Through it all, working long days and weeks, I managed to write by managing my time. Being my own boss made it possible to set my office hours, and I could write in my office without worrying about a boss sneaking in on me and chewing me out for moonlighting.

My business began to grow, and I found that I really did like advertising and marketing. Unlike working for a large corporation, I was able to make all the decisions. Some of them were bad ones, but they were mine.

My personal marketing plan was working. Best of all, my writing was beginning to pay off. In 1988 I was on a committee at New York University to discuss new courses for the 1990s. I had been teaching a course on marketing for small businesses, products and services for several years and had seen the need for a new course on personal marketing. The committee accepted my concept, and I wrote the course *Marketing Yourself* for the 1989 Fall term.

My First Book

No books were available to teach the course, and I didn't want to lecture without source material for the students, so I decided to write my own book. After all, I wanted to write, didn't I? With the exception of marketing plans, ads and commercials, I'd never written nonfiction. Short stories, novels and screenplays were what I liked to write best.

Two months before the course was to start, I became frantic. Being my own boss enabled me to take some time off. I flew to Austria and wrote every day. Drawing on my years of experience in marketing, I developed a personal marketing plan using the elements of a traditional corporate marketing plan. Six weeks later, I finished the book, *How To Market Yourself.* NYU made copies for my students for the first semester and suggested that I find a publisher. Three months later after numerous rejection slips, I found one, and the book was published exactly one year after I'd written it.

Words cannot convey the feeling of a first publication. To have someone like my work enough to pay me for it was a major milestone. Holding in my hands a book with my own name on it was—and is— an indescribable experience. If I had died at that moment, I would have died the happiest man ever. My dream had come true!

Balance

I'm now six years into my ten-year personal marketing plan and don't know if I'll ever achieve full-time writing as a profession. I have found an alternative, however, and I'm happy. Working for myself has given me more control of my time, and I have discovered how to maintain a balance of running my own business, writing and being with my family. In six years I've filled six legal-size file drawers with my writing. I just completed my 14th screenplay, and several have been optioned. This is my second nonfiction book, and I'm almost finished with a new novel that I hope will become a series. I'm ahead of my own schedule.

I'm making more money than I did in the corporate world, but money isn't the issue—happiness, fulfillment and the sense that I am doing what I really love to do are. Each year I am able to spend more time on my writing.

I've also found another unexpected bonus along the way—a second mistress—teaching. For years I taught traditional marketing courses at Parsons School of Design and New York University. I'm now an adjunct assistant professor of marketing for the Management Institute of NYU. I'm able to write and teach my own courses, and it's pure pleasure. My newest course, *Breaking the Golden*

Handcuffs, debuts in the fall of 1993. Helping others find a way out, a way to realize their dream, is my payback. It's a way to contribute that helps me feel good about myself.

I've saved the best benefit for last. When I worked in the corporate world, I was subjected to someone else's schedule. I had to travel extensively on business, sometimes being away 75 percent of the time. A major part of my decision to break the corporate bondage was to spend time with my family. I have two grown children with whom I never had the opportunity to spend time when they were small. My career kept me from really getting to know them. I left before they awoke and returned after they were asleep. My time off left me too exhausted to spend any real time with them. I was pretty much a stranger to them, a silent visitor. It's something I'll always regret.

My youngest is six now, and he's my best friend. Being out on my own allows me to schedule my time around Stefan Michael. Every morning we get up and have breakfast together. I take him to school, and I come home well before his bedtime. I know all his teachers and friends. I've never been away on business when there was a parent activity at school or a recital at his music school. I leased my office space three blocks from home, and my son can visit anytime he wants. My wife brings him, or I pick him up. Stefan even has his own desk. If I want, I can leave and meet him in the park after school. He likes to write like his daddy does and has several of his own works in progress.

Telecommuting

The nature of my business allows me to be what is known as a *telecommuter*. I maintain an office in Manhattan primarily to meet with clients and suppliers, but I really don't need one. I conduct most of my business by phone, computer modem and fax. My real office goes everywhere I go. I have a powerful notebook computer with a modem and fax board, a portable printer, a portable phone and a pager. With the aid of a full-time answering service, I am completely mobile. Both my personal and business banking are done by computer, including a line of credit for loans when I need it. My clients send their checks directly to my bank for deposit. As long as I have access to a phone link, I can conduct my business anywhere in the world. I transact business from my home, a park bench when I'm playing with my son, hotel rooms, airport departure lounges and phone booths. When I'm not working on agency business, I just switch files on the computer and start writing. My computer goes everywhere I go, giving me the flexibility to spend a lot of time with my wife and son. Many of the people I do business with assume that I am in my office on Fifth Avenue in New York when in fact I may be at home or out of the country.

For three months every summer, I take my family to our lake house in southern Austria, and my office is on a ship that sails a regular schedule between villages. Since the round trip takes a little more than four hours, this is where I do the majority of my writing. It doesn't get much better than this.

I've revealed a small part of my own experience to show you that it can be done. I hope that I've learned enough from my own successes and failures to help your journey be a little smoother. Numerous people have generously taken the time to share their experiences to help me prepare my course and this book. Now, let's get to the real heart of the matter, *your dream*.

Do It Your Way

Pursue your dream—your physical and mental health may well depend upon it. George Burns has steadfastly attributed his well-being and longevity to the fact that he has spent his life doing what he loves.

You don't have to do it my way. I chose to leave the corporate world and open a small agency in order to have control over my time to pursue writing. My career required far too much travel and extra time after hours with clients. I could never schedule any time for writing on a daily basis. There are ways that you can maintain your present profession and plan a gradual escape. In fact, I recommend it. Have patience. I know that you want to realize your dream tomorrow, but it's just not always feasible. Your biggest reward will come when you make the decision to follow your dream and chart a course to make it happen. Time moves quickly. You'll get there but only if you start taking action. The most important factor is mind-set, deciding to do it.

Once you make the decision, you must formulate a plan to make it happen. It never ceases to amaze me that some people spend more time planning their vacations than they do their careers. Why? They look at a vacation as something pleasurable and work as something unpleasant, so they try to suppress it from their consciousness. In *Tom Sawyer II,* Mark Twain tells us that "Work consists of whatever a body is obliged to do, and Play consists of whatever a body is not obliged to do."

A career can be something you feel obliged to do and look forward to each day—something to get excited about. When you figure in preparation and travel time, work usually represents the largest single segment of your time each day. Think about it! If you could spend this large block of time doing what you love to do, how happy would you be? You owe it to yourself to give it a shot.

If you're determined to break your corporate bondage, start right now. Don't put it off any longer. If you've taken the first step, deciding to do it, commit that thought to paper. Write your dream down. Spend some time getting to know it again before proceeding with the rest of this book and making your plan. If time permits, take a few days off by yourself. Use this time to visualize your dream and how it would feel to actually live it.

2

Don Quixote Complex, Different Drummers or Reality?

It's time for a reality check. Is your dream feasible? Do you have the aptitude, skills, education, training and ability? If you don't, what is needed, and how long will it take? Consider your short-term and long-term financial needs, insurance, savings and pension plans.

I find that most dreams fall into three basic categories—the *Don Quixote complex, different drummers* and *reality*. I've taught all three types of dreamers over the years, and I've learned a lot about their dreams.

Don Quixote Complex

Don Quixote dreams border on sheer fantasy. This is a catch-all category that could have many other names and subcategories since the majority of dreams fit this description. What's heartbreaking is that most people won't admit that they're chasing windmills and set themselves up for a lifetime of disappointment and frustration. A surprising number actually convince themselves that their dreams are achievable and that any disbelievers or critics become the enemy. You may be in this category and not realize it—hopefully not. Only time will tell. Sometimes luck or a quirk of fate will prove everyone wrong, but luck is not a planning tool. I define luck as being well-prepared when opportunity knocks. Photographer Ansel Adams described it extremely well in his book *Ansel Adams An Autobiography* when he told how he captured the photo, *Moonrise, Hernandez, New Mexico.*

> Driving south along the highway, I observed a fantastic scene as we approached the village of Hernandez. In the east, the moon was rising over distant clouds and snowpeaks, and in the west, the late afternoon sun glanced over a south-flowing cloud bank and blazed a brilliant white upon the crosses in the church cemetery. I steered the station wagon into the deep shoulder along the road and jumped out, scrambling to get my equipment together, yelling at Michael and Cedric to 'Get this! Get that, for God's sake! We don't have much time!' With the camera assembled and the image composed and focused, I could not find my Weston exposure meter! Behind me the sun was about to disappear behind the clouds, and I was desperate. I suddenly recalled that the luminance of the moon was 250 candles per square foot. I placed this value on Zone VII of the exposure scale; with the Wratten G (No. 15) deep yellow filter, the exposure was one second at f/32. I had no accurate reading of the shadow foreground values. After the first exposure I quickly reversed the 8 x 10 film holder to make a duplicate negative, for I instinctively knew I had visualized one of those very important images that seem prone to accident or physical defect, but as I pulled out the slide, the sunlight left the crosses, and the magical moment was gone forever.

I knew it was special when I released the shutter, but I never anticipated what its reception would be over the decades. *Moonrise, Hernandez, New Mexico* is my most well-known photograph.

Source: From *Ansel Adams: An Autobiography* by Ansel Adams and Mary Street Alinder. Copyright © 1985 by the Trustees of the Ansel Adams Publishing Rights Trust. By permission of Little, Brown & Company.

When Adams later told this story at the Museum of Modern Art, he added the line, "They say that fortune favors the prepared man." That's what this book is all about: developing a plan and following it, being prepared and making your dream come true. It won't work for you if you're in the category of chasing windmills, hoping for a stroke of luck.

I'm always frightened for those people who do strike it lucky right out of the gate, especially if they equate their overnight success with reality. As J. Christopher Herold writes in *Bonaparte in Egypt, II,* "Those who mistake their good luck for their merit are inevitably bound for disaster."

Then there are those who dream but don't do. They dream about something, talk about it and bore you to tears with it, but never do anything about making it happen—never. Deep down they probably know they're talking fantasy and realize that trying to actually carry through would reveal them as frauds. They will use any and every handy excuse. Timing is usually the best and most used excuse. The time just isn't right! They'll do it when they have some free time, some money set aside, when the kids are grown, the mortgage is paid, the right break, the right contact is made, the planets are aligned, next month, next year, when somebody recognizes their talent, whatever. These people will leave you alone if you provide the means to make their excuses disappear. They don't want to do what they've been talking about doing.

Dream oscillators may try 100 different schemes in their lifetimes without making one of them happen. Their dreams change with their underwear—sometimes faster.

Calvin and Hobbes   by Bill Watterson

They just haven't been able to clearly define what their dreams are. They usually fail because they seldom stick with anything long enough to make it happen, abandoning a half-baked idea in favor of a new and better one.

Beware of these dreamers. The majority of them will only tire you out, but a lot of them do well as opportunists and make a decent living on the fringes of the law. Some of them retire to permanent thrones in the local pub.

These people live in a fantasy world. Yes, they have clearly defined dreams. They can't be shaken or dissuaded from them; they know what they want. There's only one thing wrong with their dreams—they'll never be realized.

These folks are the saddest of the lot. They will never admit they lack what it takes to achieve their dreams. It may be a lack of talent, aptitude or skills. It's certainly not a lack of training or education—in fact, they're often quite educated. These people are not lazy. They will read every book, take every course, pursue every route of opportunity to try to fulfill their dreams. And they'll never make it. As hard as it is to do, I always try to be truthful with these people and point them in a direction more suited for them. It rarely works.

Different Drummers

People in this category are sometimes confused with the Don Quixote types. There is a real difference. Drummers generally don't talk about their dreams; they just make them happen. These are the people who change all of our lives, yet they suffer ridicule when they talk of their dreams. This category encompasses the entrepreneurs, inventors, scientists and artists of our world. Most are loners who are absolutely convinced of their mission. Different drummers will probably never read this book; they're just not the type. They go and do, charting new courses we've never dreamed of. There are no guidelines or plans for these people.

Reality

This is the category you should be in to make this book work for you. Is your dream based upon reality? People in this category have what it takes—aptitude, skills and talent. Usually they just need a push in the right direction, a determination to get on with it. Some need a helping hand, a guide to show them the way and tell them it's okay. Procrastinators are in this group also. They just keep putting their dreams off until tomorrow, and tomorrow never comes. I have a sign over my desk that I read and follow daily, "Just get the damn thing done. No excuses are accepted!"

Fear may be your biggest obstacle. Can you *really* do it? Leaving a career that pays well and represents a certain amount of security can be frightening. What if you fail? What if you've deceived yourself into thinking you have the talent and ability, and you *don't*? Fear alone may be tightening your corporate bondage. A certain amount of fear is healthy. It will help you analyze your dream and make sure you've based it on reality. If fear is immobilizing you, read Chapter 4, "Your Personal and Financial Health." If you're having trouble defining your dream, read my previous book, *How To Market Yourself.* It will help you prepare a personal marketing plan based upon your ability and talent, likes and dislikes.

Fame and Fortune

The last category I personally consider useless but feel compelled to mention anyway. Is your dream just to be rich or famous? I don't even consider these dreams worthy of pursuing. What would you do if suddenly you became wealthy or famous overnight? What if you inherited a lot of money or won the lottery? Having money does not guarantee happiness. I've met many idle, rich, moneyed people who are incredibly unhappy. Some people have one goal, making money. They equate money with status, power and pride. They are constantly restless. Ego, pride, headlines and fame are their only pursuits. They are the most insecure people I've ever met, empty shells that can never be filled.

Then there are the people who want to be famous. They equate fame with happiness. They want a quick fix—the glamour without the work. Every semester I get at least one of these people in my course, *Marketing Yourself.* They come to the first class and find out they have to do some work for themselves. They're shocked and don't show up for the rest of the course. A few of them gravitate toward a profession that will give them visibility and exposure, such as acting. Some of them make it and create their own corporate bondage.

Why Do You Want To Change Careers?

Change for the Sake of Change?

"I'm sick and tired of my job. I'm fed up with my life—I need a change!"

"To what?"

"Anything!"

This state of mind seems to strike most of us at least once in mid-life. There must be a genetic code that triggers this hopeless dissatisfaction with our lives. Thankfully, it usually passes quickly, and we get on with it. In the majority of cases, it's brought on by extreme fatigue or stress—sometimes by an illness or boredom itself. Whatever the cause, a vacation, a rest or the passing of time usually gets us back on course, and we're reasonably happy again.

With some people, the state of mind intensifies, becoming an overwhelming force that drives them to take action—any kind of action. Many psychiatrists describe

19

this as a mid-life crisis, and it seems to strike people in their mid-to-late 40s. Men in particular are susceptible at about age 40 when they may experience *second puberty*. They begin to question where they are in life with their careers. Their personal appearance becomes important again, and they strive to look 20. The mid-life crisis has driven people to divorce for no apparent reason and has caused senior executives to throw their careers away while they go and *smell the flowers*. Such a crisis involves change for the sake of change. It has no direction or planning behind it, and it's dangerous. Its trail is littered with broken families, wasted dreams, substance abuse, severe depression and sometimes suicide.

Get a Game Plan

Making a change *just* to make a change is not breaking away from corporate bondage. You'll need a well-thought-out game plan to make sure that you've explored in detail what you really want and have thoroughly examined your current dilemma. Your present dissatisfaction with your career or your life may be rooted in other causes. You may very well be in the right career and not need to make a change in your dream at all. The cause of your unhappiness may be only as deep as the company or people you work for. It could involve the size of the company—too small or too large—or it may be the city you live in or even the climate. The key here is to find out if you really want to make a major life change and, if so, to what.

Another dangerous trap people fall into is looking for someone else to change their lives. It never works. Only you can change your life and be happy with the results. If you're not happy, it isn't someone else's fault, and another person is not going to make it better. The first thing you have to evaluate is what you want. Define it. Once you do, you can start changing the circumstances to achieve it.

It's not that unusual to put together a game plan and decide not to change careers. This doesn't mean the game plan was a wasted effort. If anything, such planning refreshes your outlook and reinforces your determination to move forward. It allows you to recognize and examine your strengths and weaknesses and take advantage of the knowledge to move at a faster pace to achieve your dream. It adds a planning tool to your life and puts you in control. Often it is a reconfirmation of your original goals that just need some fine-tuning.

I've counseled a number of people in the past who were absolutely on the right career path. A step-by-step process of self-examination helped them to recognize other areas of their lives that were bothering them and dragging them down. The game plan they developed helped them *cut down the weeds* in their mental garden and eliminate the unnecessary.

Be Prepared for Criticism

Almost everyone I've interviewed agrees that it's probably not a good idea to discuss your dream with others until you are certain that you are going to pursue it. It is especially important to avoid discussing such things with your employer or fellow employees. This could lead to someone else breaking your corporate bondage before you are prepared.

Your family and friends may feel threatened by your decision, and you must have a clearly defined plan before you break the news. If they know it's something that you really want and you've planned how to make it happen (especially the financial end), you'll have a much better chance of eliciting their support.

Even so, you may find members of your family not being supportive. They may feel threatened by such a sudden (to them) move on your part. If you've been earning a substantial salary and your lifestyle has been quite comfortable, your family may worry about going backward. Some of these anxieties can be alleviated if you are mentally prepared in advance and armed with a well-thought-out plan.

Be aware of family or friends who may try to talk you out of your pursuit. Try to determine what their motives are. It's not uncommon for some people to feel threatened by your move because it causes them to question their own lives. If you make the break and become successful, they may feel more insecure. Undoubtedly someone will try to make you *come to your senses*. If you are sure of your dream, this shouldn't cause you to start hedging. If you start questioning yourself after people try to talk you out of your dream, then you really may not be ready to make the move.

If you do decide to follow your dream and you are in your 40s, someone will probably accuse you of going through a mid-life crisis or second puberty. Some may even feel that you need to check into a mental institution. The whole point here is that if you are prepared for criticism in advance, you'll handle it much better. If you don't encounter it, fine. At least you've armed yourself. . . just in case.

Your Personal and Financial Health

Your Personal Health

If you are feeling at a complete loss and have no sense of what is causing your dissatisfaction with your job or your life, consider seeking professional help. It's not a sign of weakness to go into therapy; actually the reverse is true. Being able to admit that you need help is actually a strength. Trying to "be strong," carrying the burden alone, is a weakness. I look at therapy as a powerful tool and have used it often. In fact, it became the turning point in my life, allowing me to start pursuing my dream.

I highly recommend getting a complete physical examination to rule out any medical problems that could be contributing to your stressed-out feelings. Other factors, such as poor nutrition, bad eating habits, inadequate rest and lack of exercise, can contribute to a run-down, *sick and tired* feeling.

Proper nutrition, good health and methods of coping with stress will either make or break your ability to function at optimal levels.

The Importance of Good Health

Consider the days when your mind is sharp, your mood is level and your decision-making is clear and concise. These are the days when your energy is limitless, you could lick the world and you seem to get mountains of work done with ease. Wouldn't it be wonderful if you could make every day that way?

One of the best books I've read on good health in many years is *The Executive Success Diet*, by June Roth, M. S. and Harvey M. Ross, M. D. With their permission, I've included the outlines of "Eight Fast Steps to Health Control." For a complete guide to increasing your energy and productivity, I recommend that you read the book in its entirety.

Step 1. Increase Your Intake of Complex Carbohydrates.

- There are two kinds of carbohydrates: simple and complex.

- Simple carbohydrates are sugar, syrup and honey. They are metabolized and enter the blood swiftly, causing rapid increases and decreases in blood sugar levels that affect mood, ability to concentrate and energy levels.

- It's best to avoid simple carbohydrates whenever possible. This is difficult to do because they are hidden throughout the food supply, sometimes in the most unsuspected places. Simple carbohydrates are the *bad guys* of wise nutrition.

- Complex carbohydrates are the *good guys*. They are found in whole grains (cereals, bread, pasta, brown rice, kasha), vegetables and fruits. They are metabolized and enter the blood slowly, causing steady maintenance of blood-sugar levels.

- Complex carbohydrates are also a good source of fiber in the diet. Fiber provides bulk needed for healthy bowel regularity and is considered to be an important weapon against colon cancer.

- Grains in complex carbohydrates provide a rich assortment of B vitamins and many essential minerals.

- Vegetable complex carbohydrates provide a nutrient pool of vitamins A and C. All vegetables are rich in C. The dark yellow and dark green vegetables also offer good sources of A.

- Fruits, especially the citrus fruits (orange, grapefruit, lemon, lime), provide vitamin C. They also supply essential minerals, such as potassium.

- A large variety of complex carbohydrates in the diet will give you an excellent reserve of glycogen—your bank of energy.

- Carbohydrates have only four calories per gram, as does protein. Fat has nine calories per gram.

- At least 55 percent of the diet should be in the form of complex carbohydrates for optimal nutrition. This means that in a 1,500-calorie day, 825 calories should be in the form of grains, vegetables and fruit.

Step 2. Beware of Excess Fat Consumption.

- Fat has 100 calories per level tablespoon, whether from butter, margarine, oil, shortening or animal fat.

- Saturated fat from animal sources is implicated in coronary artery disease. This includes the fat in beef, pork, lamb, poultry, fish and butter, and the butterfat in whole milk and dairy products. Limit portions to four-ounce or five-ounce servings.

- Unsaturated fat from vegetable sources is considered a better choice if you are concerned about high blood-cholesterol levels. Corn oil, safflower oil, cotton oil and vegetable oil blends provide unsaturated fats. Exceptions are coconut oil and palm oil, which have a higher degree of saturation.

- It takes twice as long to digest fat as it does protein and carbohydrate foods.

- Every gram of fat has nine calories as compared to four per gram for protein and carbohydrate foods.

- The medical and nutritional communities agree that an intake of 30 percent or less of fat in your total calorie count is a wise objective. This means that in a 1,500-calorie day, no more than 450 calories should be derived from all forms of fat intake.

Step 3. Eat Adequate Protein.

- Protein is an important and necessary substance in the maintenance of good health and in the growth and repair of all body tissues.

- Protein is necessary for the formation of hormones, which control such body functions as growth, metabolism and sexual development.

- Protein is an essential element in forming enzymes. Enzymes are needed to convert the food you eat into the nutrients the body requires. Enzymes are like the workers in a large corporation—each has a specific job to do, and if even one is missing, malfunction can occur.

- Amino acids are provided by protein. Of the 22 amino acids necessary to human function, there are 8 the body cannot produce by itself. These eight are called *essential amino acids*. They must be consumed as complete protein in the foods you eat.

- Meat, poultry, fish, eggs and dairy products provide complete essential amino acids in the diet.

Grains and legumes each have some (but different ones) of the essential amino acids. When served together and digested at the same time, they bond into complete essential amino acids as well. If eaten at separate meals, the grains (wheat, corn, barley, rye, oats) and legumes (any beans, peas, or peanut butter) will not provide this same quality of complete protein.

• Examples of the grain and legume combination are chili beans on rice, succotash (lima beans and corn) and a peanut butter sandwich on whole-wheat bread.

• Most meat, poultry, fish, eggs and dairy products also have a good proportion of fat in them. This makes it necessary to select lean meat (such as veal, filet mignon, well-trimmed round steak and well-trimmed shoulder or baby lamb chops). Remove poultry skin after cooking it; cook fish without additional fat; limit eggs; and use only skim or low-fat dairy products.

• Protein deficiency affects growth and tissue development.

• In times of stress from illness or surgery, extra protein is needed to rebuild the body's tissues.

• About 15 percent of the daily diet should be comprised of protein. The recommended daily allowance (as determined by The National Research Council Food and Nutrition Board) for protein for healthy adults is 44–56 grams, while the Council sets the figure at 70 grams for an adult man and 60 for an adult woman. Most Americans manage to eat a great deal more protein than the recommended allowance.

Step 4. Learn How To Detect Hidden Salt.

• One level teaspoon of salt contains 2,300 milligrams of sodium.

- Sodium is also found naturally in vegetables, fruits, grains, meat, poultry and fish in varying amounts.

- If you eat unsalted food and avoid hidden sodium in manufactured food products, you will probably be ingesting about 2,500 milligrams of sodium— just the amount your body needs to function well.

- There is no need to cook with salt or to add it to your food at the table. The desire for flavor can be supplied with the deft use of herbs, spices and other seasoning agents.

- Even if you are exercising and sweating profusely, there is no need to take salt tablets. Just sprinkle a little salt over your next meal to make up for the loss of sodium through perspiration.

- Excessive salt in the diet interferes with the absorption and utilization of protein.

- Sodium and potassium control the fluid balance within the body. If there is excessive salt intake, too much potassium may be excreted in the urine, which leads to impaired muscle function.

- Excess sodium intake can cause fluid retention, which in turn can cause high blood pressure, which in turn can cause a stroke.

- Low sodium intake can alleviate the symptoms of edema (swelling of body tissues that are saturated with fluid) caused by excess salt consumption.

- When dining in a restaurant, know that the prepared soups are generally high in salt content. Also vegetables that are kept in steaming trays, prepared meat dishes such as stews and pasta sauces are generally high in salt.

- When ordering a sandwich, avoid *deli* meats such as corned beef, pastrami and luncheon meats because of their extremely high sodium content. Skip the pickle—it has been soaked in brine.

• Canned soups are notoriously high in sodium content unless they are labeled as low-sodium products.

• Frozen dinners usually are very high in sodium content, as are most packaged convenience foods and mixes.

• Canned tomato and tomato-combination juices are high-sodium fare. Remember that most carbonated beverages also have sodium, except for those that are clearly marked *low-salt* or *no salt.*

• When you avoid extra salting of food, your taste buds adapt to the change in three to six weeks, and your palate will be able to detect foods that have been oversalted.

• It is a good plan not to pick up the salt shaker unless you have experienced heavy sweating from exercise or a fever.

Step 5. Learn the Speed Method of Calorie Control.

• Calories do count. 3,500 excess calories will give you a one-pound weight gain. 3,500 fewer calories than you need will give you a one-pound weight loss. Just 500 extra calories each day can add up to 3,500 calories in a week—or a one pound weight gain.

• Most people become confused when trying to accurately add up every single bite of food to get a daily total of caloric intake. It's best to tackle calories in round numbers and to get an approximate total, to keep control of how much you are eating in relation to how much energy you are expending. If you can keep these amounts in reasonable balance, you will not add to the fat warehouses of the body, but you will provide adequate nutrients to keep the body in good health.

Step 6. Learn When To Use Nutritional Supplements.

- Nutritional supplements may be used as insurance by a healthy person to help prevent illness. When used for this purpose the dosages do not usually have to be large and are determined by the individual based on personal health experiences.

- Nutritional supplements may be used as a treatment or part of the treatment plan for some illnesses. When used in this manner they should be prescribed by a qualified physician or nutritionist.

- The theoretical *balanced diet* would, by definition, supply all needed nutrients for most people. But who eats a perfectly balanced diet? The U.S. Department of Agriculture estimates that about 50 percent of all people in the United States actually eat less than the recommended amounts of all nutrients.

- The recommended amounts of nutrients frequently change, leading one to believe (and rightly so) that such a recommendation is more arbitrary than scientific.

- The RDA (recommended daily allowance) is not necessarily the optimum daily allowance. The RDA may prevent deficiency diseases, but it does little to maintain optimum health.

- Vitamin requirements vary from person to person, and individual requirements change from time to time, depending upon stress level.

- The nutrients, vitamins and minerals in foods vary from season to season and are highly dependent upon farming techniques, fertilization methods and utilization of the land.

- Nutrient content of food is depleted over time and during processing. Processing of foods to lengthen shelf life, prevent spoilage and allow shipping from farm to market is a fact of life, but processing is not accomplished without loss of nutritional quality.

- Another form of processing that robs foods of nutrients is overcooking.

- Vitamins derived from natural sources are not superior to man-made vitamins, with the possible exception of vitamin A and vitamin C. The vitamin C from natural sources contains more of the C-complex than the man-made ascorbic acid.

- Vitamins and minerals work together as a team to enable the many complex chemical reactions in our bodies to take place at every instant. Vitamins are generally classified according to their ability to dissolve in water or fat. The fat-soluble vitamins are stored in the fat of the body. The water-soluble vitamins are not stored.

Step 7. Control Your Physical Profile.

You should regularly schedule routine, general physical examinations.

- Blood tests are done to assist in the diagnosis of disease, to determine the general state of health before symptoms of illness occur and to follow the progress of a disease process.

- The results of blood tests should be consistent with other clinical facts concerning the patient. Laboratories are not infallible and are subject to human as well as mechanical error. Questionable, unexpected results should be rechecked.

- There are no absolute normal levels. When determining the significance of any test, be certain that the normal ranges for the laboratory are known. This is especially important when comparing results from one laboratory to another.

- The significance of some abnormal laboratory results must be determined by a consideration of all information available, which includes a careful history and other laboratory tests and diagnostic procedures, such as X-rays.

- Hundreds of blood tests are possible, but certain routine screening tests are done at the time of a general physical examination and usually during hospitalization. In addition to the routine testing, specific tests may be done to determine hormone levels, the efficiency of the immune system, drug levels, vitamin and mineral levels and amino-acid content. Specialized tests are done only if the condition or history suggests an abnormality in those specific areas.

- Any part of the body may be subject to laboratory scrutiny. Hair, cerebrospinal fluid, sputum, blood, urine, feces and bone marrow are all examined for different reasons.

Step 8. Learn Emotional-Stress-Reduction Techniques.

- Emotional stress varies from individual to individual. What is stressful to one person is of no consequence to another.

- Stress is more apt to persist when the cause of stress is repressed or hidden from you. Fighting an unrecognized enemy is impossible.

- Stress is more serious if alternatives to problems aren't recognized.

- Stress is more difficult to manage if health is poor or less than optimum.

Handling Stress

- Stay healthy. Only then do you have the equipment, the brain power and physical power necessary to recognize, analyze and manage problems. Staying healthy involves inheriting the right genes (you can't do much about this one), exercise, diet and attitude.

- Stress may be reduced by a careful analysis of a problem.

"Oh God, grant me the SERENITY to accept the things I cannot change, the COURAGE to change the things I can and the WISDOM to know the difference." [from *The Serenity Prayer*]

- Hard work is not stress. It's fun to work hard on things you've got under control. What does cause stress is loss of control.

- When you raise your control level, you lower the element of stress. Setting goals for yourself and achieving them can help give you the control over your life that will help reduce stress.

Source: McGraw-Hill, Inc. Reprinted with permission.

You are happier in life if you know what your goals are.

Many stress-reducing techniques are available; finding the right one is a matter of taste and choice.

Before embarking on any major life change, give yourself the edge of starting out at the top of your form. Take the time to analyze why you want to make a change and what that change should be. Don't make the mistake of making a change just for the sake of a change. It invariably leads to a new set of problems and possibly more corporate bondage.

Recognizing that you need some kind of change in your life can be a healthy state of mind if utilized properly. Take the time to examine the things you really want to change. Find out what you really want out of life. What would make you happy? Map out a plan to make it happen.

Your Financial Health

Your financial health is just as important as your physical health. Nothing causes stress faster than money problems. All your time and energy must be devoted to pursuing your dream. Work on this area until you feel you are in control and know exactly where you stand financially. The following advice is from *Kiplinger's Personal Finance Magazine*:

> No matter how unhappy you may be, the thought of making a radical change is frightening. To cut down on the feeling that you may be jumping off a cliff, here's what to do *before* you make the change.

> *Free Up Cash.* Refinance your mortgage to reduce payments. Raise the deductibles on your homeowner's, auto and health insurance. Get quick cash from a loan against cash-value life insurance.

> *Apply for a Home-Equity Loan.* While you still have the income to support repayment, apply for a home-equity line of credit. Set it aside for emergency, short-term personal or business use.

> *Rework Your Benefits.* If you switch to part-time work, you may qualify for medical, dental, life and long-term disability coverage under group plans, especially if you work 20 hours or more a week. You'll probably have to pay at least part of the cost. If you quit your job to start your own business, you will have to work out coverage individually.

> *Health Insurance.* The best solution is to get coverage under a working spouse's company policy, even if you have to pay for family coverage. If that is not an option, group coverage will continue for at least 18 months after you leave a company with 20 or more employees (but you'll likely pay the whole premium). Use that time to find replacement coverage. Look first for individual coverage or a good policy from an affinity group. If that fails, you may be able to convert from your group policy to an individual policy.

> *Disability Insurance.* Many companies provide this at no cost to their employees. Typical group policies replace 60 percent of salary. Normally, you

can't take this policy with you when you leave the company.

You'll have the most trouble getting coverage if your new venture doesn't directly relate to your prior experience, says William Payne, an insurance consultant with PRW Associates, in Braintree, Massachusetts. And if you start a home-based business of any kind, you may not be able to get any individual coverage.

You may be able to avoid these complications by pulling out of your group policy and buying individual coverage before you leave your job. You can take this coverage with you, but premiums can be expensive. For a 40-year-old nonsmoker (male or female) earning $45,000 a year as a banker, an individual policy paying $2,550 in monthly benefits after a 90-day waiting period would cost $1,152 per year with Unum, one of the nation's largest disability insurance carriers. The same policy for a 50-year-old nonsmoker costs $1,776 a year.

Life Insurance. Many company group term life insurance policies can be converted into individual coverage when you leave your job. Consider term insurance for your spouse if you'll be depending more heavily upon his or her income.

Pension. Lump-sum pensions should be rolled over to an IRA. If you use the money for your business you will not only be taxed on it, if younger than 55 you will also be hit with a 10 percent penalty or more.

Source: Adapted from the June 1992 issue of *Kiplinger's Personal Finance Magazine.* Copyright © 1992 by The Kiplinger Washington Editors, Inc.

Your personal and financial health are very important areas that require considerable attention not only now, before you make a change, but on a continuing basis. Both are integral parts of your plan and go hand-in-hand. Health problems can create financial problems, and financial problems can cause health problems. Pay attention!

5

What if Someone Else Breaks Your Corporate Bondage?

Corporate bondage may be broken by someone other than yourself. You could be going along in your successfully unhappy state, and one day your boss calls you in for a little chat. You're not being fired—today people in your position are never fired—but you're being transferred into the new legion of people who are in *outplacement*. There's always a *logical* reason: The company is downsizing. You are overqualified for the *new* company. A person of your experience and talent would be unhappy. The company is merging or being bought out, and your position and staff are a duplication of the new parent company's staff. Your division is being eliminated along with several others, and there's no place to put you. The company is filing for bankruptcy, and the courts want to see an immediate reorganization.

It doesn't matter what they call it, you're being fired—canceled. What are you going to do now? You weren't happy with the job, but you wanted it to be your choice when you left. What if you're lucky and land a new job quickly? Will it happen again? If you get a similar position with a similar company, aren't you just signing up for more corporate bondage?

The first thing you should do is *nothing*. Don't panic and send out 1,000 resumes. Look at this seemingly disastrous incident as a possible *golden opportunity*. Instead of feeling sorry for yourself, let your new situation be the force that moves you. Stop the chronic procrastinating that is plaguing you. Maybe it's time to start that new business you've dreamed about for years.

Time To Plan

Quickly do a personal financial statement. How much money do you have in reserve? What can you do immediately to cut down on expenses? How much time can you buy for yourself?

Make a game plan for your dream. Take a week off to do nothing but work on your plan using the outlines in later chapters. Don't make any moves toward finding a new job yet. If nothing else, the week of working on your dream will take your mind off the disaster. You'll be able to think with improved clarity after doing your game plan.

You might find it impossible to make your escape right away. Financial situations probably require that you become employed again as quickly as possible. Start your job search with a different outlook. Look at immediate employment as short-term, a way to pay the bills. Maybe you'll want to take a different approach to the kind of employment you seek, knowing that it will be an interim step on the way to pursuing your dream.

Many companies today provide outplacement assistance for employees who have been let go. Outplacement professionals will concentrate on helping you find a job similar to your last one. You can use them for an added bonus. If you are really determined to escape from corporate bondage, tell your counselors what your dream is. Have them test you for what you really want to do, not the job you just vacated. They can determine your aptitude and talent—whether you have the right stuff. They will help you build your game plan and list the things you must do to make it happen. You still may have to accept a job similar to your last one, but you'll be armed with a game plan to make your dream come true.

If your company does not provide outplacement services and you can afford them yourself, now may be an excellent time to seek out a counselor before you plunge into serious job hunting.

What if You Were Fired?

If you were fired—really fired—for a reason, take the time to analyze why it happened. Was it justified? Be honest. If it was justified, the reason may be that you've been harboring a deep-rooted dislike for what you do. Instead of spending time feeling sorry for yourself, start making a game plan. If your firing was unjustified, don't spend time being angry. It's never productive. Work on your dream.

Look at being fired as an opportunity, an outside push that could be just what you need to get going. I've met many people through the years who have told me that the best thing that ever happened to them occurred when they were let go from a job they didn't like. Granted they weren't thrilled when it first happened, but being fired got them jump-started into finally doing something.

Part 2

Your Personal Plan

"It's the old story. I was in the middle of a successful acting career when I was bitten by the accounting bug."

Source: Drawing by Leo Cullum; © 1992 The New Yorker Magazine, Inc.

6

Personal Dream Assessment

Your Personal Plan

Take your personal dream plan very seriously. If you spend the time well and expend the effort, it will change your life forever. Start by committing your dream to paper today. Your goal should be well-defined before you proceed beyond this point.

If your dream is to be a writer, what kind of writer do you want to be? There are many categories, such as reporting, short stories, fiction, nonfiction, screenplays, novels and so on. If you want to open a small business, what type of business? You must be very clear. If you don't know the destination, there's no way you'll ever be able to chart a course to get there. If your dream is vague, take some time to think it through. If you've definitely made the decision to escape from corporate bondage, don't make the mistake of putting on a similar pair of handcuffs.

Your personal plan requires a lot of hard work, and you should set aside time to work on it—without distractions or interruptions. I personally recommend taking a vacation by yourself to a quiet location. If this proves impossible, try to take one or two days off by yourself. The main point here is not to rush your personal plan. This is a major life change. Treat it as the most important thing you'll ever do.

Your personal dream plan consists of seven phases or steps:

1. Personal dream assessment
2. The right stuff
3. Your current dilemma
4. Making your game plan
5. Putting your plan into action
6. Monitoring your progress
7. The great escape

Don't skip any of these steps. Each one is there for a very good reason. These steps have been field tested by many people, myself included. Work on each one thoroughly before proceeding to the next one. I know that you might be strongly tempted to go right to step seven, your escape. Don't do it unless you win the lottery.

I was accused of going to step seven when I left CBS and made my decision not to return to a corporate marketing job. But remember what my dream is—to be a full-time writer. My personal plan allowed for ten years to achieve this dream. I opened a small business as my bridge to this dream, and my small business is in a field that I worked in for more than 25 years. My small business allows me the freedom to plan my work, family and writing time. I'm still working on my great escape—in 1996. I am able to write more each year than I had expected. If enough people buy this book, I might make my escape ahead of schedule. Spread the word!

Personal Dream Assessment

You know what your dream is, right? Do you know what living it entails? A surprising number of people don't. Thorough research is needed for two very good reasons. The first one is to assess whether this is really what you want. Are there some aspects of this new career path and life that you might consider unpleasant? If so, can you live with them? This is a crucial step; be meticulous. And second, do you know what the basic requirements are? What is needed to succeed? How long will it take?

Research

The word *research* intimidates almost everyone but professional researchers. Research is nothing more than finding out as much as you can about something, particularly the information you need to make decisions. It is very important that you spend enough time on this step and are thorough in gathering everything available that is relevant to your goal or dream. Try to get your hands on everything. Don't stop to judge anything at this point. You'll have time later to decide what's useful or not. You can never gather enough information, but too little can be disastrous and lead you to make wrong assumptions.

The Library

Information can be gathered from a variety of sources, but your best and least expensive initial source will be the public library. Almost every large city has a main library with a business section that can help you locate information on career/professional goals. Most of these business sections have business directories, periodicals and recent business publications, with access to microfilm storage and computer-stored information. If you are lucky enough to have a library that indices on computer, the computer can help you search out the sources you need. If you are not accustomed to using a library, don't be intimidated. The librarians know how to access the information you need and are happy to help you. Just ask.

A second good source is the microfilm library of your local newspaper. If you have a personal computer, or access to one, you can also buy a modem and subscribe to numerous on-line information sources.

Personal Contact

As stated earlier, research is just information. Common sense will dictate many ways you can get this information. You can acquire a lot of it by observing and asking questions. Talk to people who are in the field you want to pursue. If you know someone in that field, try to get close to them. If you don't know anyone, ask friends if they do. Or approach a stranger. Write a letter first. State that your objective is to enter the field that they are successful in and that you would like to seek their advice. Make a long list of these people, and write to them all. Allow for a reasonable amount of time—several weeks at least—and follow up with a phone call.

I've always found that writing first is the best way to contact someone I haven't met. It then gives you a reason to call to see if the person received your letter. Don't be concerned with being rejected. You'll be surprised at the number of people who respond if they have the time. The ones who reject or are rude to you are not the ones you want to talk to anyway. They're probably not happy with themselves or are too caught up in their ego and pride. You want the winners.

Talk to as many people as you can. Ask them to tell you about their profession—how they got started, what their jobs are like and what their recommendations would be for someone like yourself who is considering entering their field. Take notes. Most of all, listen carefully. People who are successful in the field you are planning on pursuing can tell you almost everything you need to know. You may be fortunate enough to meet some new friends or receive tutoring and help to get you on your way.

Read biographies and autobiographies of people you feel have made it. Check out back issues of industry publications that may feature interviews or profiles of people in the field. Almost every industry has one or more publications devoted to it. Ask your librarian for help in locating them.

If your dream is to own your own business, concentrate your research on businesses of a similar nature. Again, the business section of your public library should be the first place you check. Next, make a list of all the companies in your city that are in the field you wish to enter. Visit these companies—first as a customer. Your goal here is to observe. Try to judge which companies are the most successful and which ones aren't. Both examples will give you valuable information. Learn from the success and failure of others.

Cull the list down to six—three you consider successful, three you consider borderline. Try to meet and interview the owners. This may prove to be a little difficult since your dream, if implemented, will make you a competitor in some sense. Try anyway—the information gained will prove useful. Another approach is to observe a few businesses outside the area where you plan to locate. This removes the problem of the owner feeling threatened by you as potential competition.

Carefully check out the city, state and federal regulations and tax situations related to your business. I recommend that you seek professional help here since some businesses can be very complicated in licensing and taxes. An investment of a few hours' time with a tax specialist and a lawyer who handles small businesses may save you a lot of headaches and money. This step will also allow you to get a firm grip on the finances you may need for your start up. A lawyer can advise you on incorporation matters. If a partnership is involved, it is crucial that a partnership agreement be drawn up before you start. The battlefield of small businesses is littered with deaths due to a partner disagreement after the businesses became successful. Be meticulous in deciding who is responsible for what and how partners are to be compensated.

Don't Skip the Basics

Many good books are available on starting a small business, some specific to particular industries. Study these books. If your small business is going to be something new and there is no competition to evaluate or books to study, you still need to know the basics of how to structure and market a small business. Your business will fall into an existing category, such as—manufacturing a product, wholesaling, retailing or a service industry. Don't skip the basics. Invest the time before you start your business. Many of my former students at NYU have been owners who sought help *after* their business started to fail. Playing catch-up is no fun.

Spend a lot of time on the research step. Your objective is very clear. Don't just dream about what you would like to be; become intimate with it. Get to really know it, and you'll be well-prepared when you start making your game plan. You'll have all the information you need to determine what you'll have to get done and how long it may take. Hopefully, your research efforts will shore up your determination to get on with making your dream come true.

Doing all this research may seem like a lot of hard work and take an inordinate amount of time. *Don't* treat it lightly. Winners know what they're getting into. It's better to know what's in store before you make the plunge than to scramble around when you're in the thick of running your new business.

I've included some biographies in Part 3 that show you how some people have broken their corporate bondage. I could not possibly have included people from every field of endeavor within the scope of this book. Overall, however, I feel that most of the people profiled have one thing in common that all of us can learn from—the determination to free themselves from bondage and make their dreams happen. Their stories are truly inspirational. Once you have freed yourself and followed your dream, *your* story will become an inspiration to others.

7

The Right Stuff

Breather #1

Take a breather. If you've done a thorough job of researching, you should have a mountain of data to analyze. When people hear the words *analyze* or *analysts*, a curtain often drops over their eyes. These terms are unfamiliar to many of us. Analyzing means nothing more than taking all the research you've gathered and looking through it to see what you should do.

Now it's time to sift through all the research information you've gathered and throw out or remove from sight everything that is unnecessary. Let's say that you've ended up with information about 20 or more businesses similar to your dream business. After evaluating all this information on your first pass, narrow the list down to the six you want to study in-depth, then dispose of all unnecessary information. Having it around tends to make your task look more formidable and can lead to confusion.

Double-check all your research. Make sure that you know the source and validity of the information as you analyze it. This is a rule to remember before you use any information to make important judgments.

Can you make valid assumptions from the research? Does the research provide enough information to answer all the wants, needs and demands of your dream? If it doesn't, dig deeper until it does. You should periodically review your assumptions and update them. Continue to do more research for your dream on a regular basis.

Re-analyze your dream based on the information you have gathered. Stop, look and listen often!

Stop!

It's time to stop for a short while and walk away from all the research. Let the subconscious mind work on it and digest it.

Look!

Read through the statement of your dream, and analyze the cut-down version of the research and information you have gathered.

Listen!

Listen to what your statement says. Is your dream still what you want—*really*? Your research will tell you if it is achievable. If not, now is the time to rethink your dream.

Can You Make Your Dream Come True?

Do you have the *right stuff*? Do you have what it takes to make your dream come true? The purpose of doing all the research was to give you the opportunity to have hard data on what it takes to make your dream come true.

Being very careful and honest with yourself, do you have the brains, the aptitude and the talent to make your dream come true? You either do or you don't. Many professions, such as modeling and acting, attract an immense number of people who have the looks, but they don't have *talent*. Many of these people suffer from the Don Quixote complex, but a larger number have been misguided by well-meaning family or friends who have constantly told them, "With your looks, you should be in modeling or acting." Some parents want to identify with fame so much that they push their children into the field when they can barely walk or talk. It's unfortunate and heartbreaking to see some of these untalented kids suffer rejection after rejection. Some of them are scarred for life.

Unfortunately, an entire industry is devoted to exploiting the Don Quixotes. Be on the alert for these companies. Make sure that you deal with only the many reputable companies that will be honest about your ability and talent. The others—the exploiters—will gladly take your money for training and building portfolios without any concern about whether or not you have *talent*. The same applies to all endeavors involving the *creative* careers. Art schools, writing schools and all forms of specialized vocational schools should be checked out carefully before you sign any contracts. The good ones will evaluate your ability and talent before admitting you.

Be careful if you are being goaded or pushed by well-meaning family or friends into believing that you have the goods to make it. If you are unsure about your abilities, ask a professional to help you make the evaluation. This person must be a third party who doesn't know you well. You want an honest professional, not someone who doesn't want to hurt your feelings by dashing your dream. Don't always trust the evaluation of only one professional. Get second, even third or fourth opinions. This is your life. There's no time for pussyfooting around.

On the other hand, be just as leery of family or friends who scoff at your dream. Generally, they are not qualified to make a judgment of your ability or talent. In fact, it may be in their best interests that you not make any change in your life. It can be just as scary for them, even more so. Maybe Mom wanted you to be a doctor, Dad wanted you to run the family business or your spouse wants you to continue being a well-paid stockbroker to support your current lifestyle. Whatever your dream, you can always find an infinite number of people ready to compare it to *Freddy's Nightmare*.

The point here is simple. Make sure that you really have the right stuff to make your dream come true. Assuming you have the brains, aptitude and talent, you can obtain everything else. Education, training and practice are key. It's now only a matter of determining what you need and how long it will take to get it. This will comprise the formulation of your game plan.

Strengths and Weaknesses

This step comes after both your dream assessment and the right stuff for a very good reason. Now that you've identified your dream and researched it, this exercise will help you decide if you can achieve your dream with what you've got and what you can acquire. See Figure 7.1 on page 58 for a sample evaluation checklist.

Make two lists: one for strengths/likes and one for weaknesses/dislikes. Under "strengths," list what you consider your most valuable assets.

Strengths

Examples:

- Character traits
- Natural talents and abilities
- Appearance and body structure
- Scholastic achievements
- Career achievements
- Social status
- Finances

Basically, enumerate the things you have going for you or things that you are naturally good at—mathematics, manual dexterity, endurance, sports, organization abilities, leadership abilities, evaluating, inventing, finding solutions to problems, etc.

Things You Like

Next, list all the things you like to do in all of these categories of strengths. What are your greatest loves?

Rate your strengths and loves starting with one. Determine to make your dream plan brilliant by utilizing your strengths and the things you like to do best to achieve your career goal.

The following are some good examples:

- *Your strength is tennis, and you love to play tennis*: You should consider becoming a tennis pro. If you are not good enough, too old or don't have the financial backing to become a pro, you could become a trainer. Or you could run a tennis school or club or even consider owning one.
- *You are a great cook, and you love cooking*: You should consider pursuing a career as a great chef, opening your own restaurant or writing cookbooks.
- *You are a good observer of details, and you love movies*: You should consider becoming a movie critic.

What strengths can you work on and make stronger? What strengths can you combine?

Weaknesses

What do you consider to be your greatest weaknesses? What traits hold you back in life and keep you from accomplishing your dream? Are you too shy? Are you always late for meetings or appointments? Are you disorganized or sloppy? Do you have very little time for other people or their problems? Are you a poor listener? Are you aloof? Do you smoke too much? Do you drink too much or use drugs? Are you too lazy? Do you have any phobias?

The list can go on and on. Try to identify the traits that you dislike in yourself. Which ones are your co-workers, friends and family constantly pointing out to you? Which ones are holding you back? Which ones can you work on and change? Which ones do you *want* to change?

This is a touchy and personal area. No one is telling you to stop anything. No one is criticizing anything you do. But if you are dedicated to making your dream come true, you should consider *all* your weaknesses to determine whether any of them are holding you back. If any of your weaknesses are beyond or out of your control, consider finding outside help or counseling.

Things You Dislike

What really turns you off? Study your dream carefully before you make it final. If there is something you really hate about your dream profession, think twice about pursuing it. If it's just a minor dislike or annoyance, ask yourself if you can live with it or at least accept it.

For example, you don't like cocktail parties, but your dream profession requires that you attend a lot of them to be successful. Instead of hating cocktail parties, can you try to relax and use them for another purpose—like meeting new friends or people watching? The big question is whether attending these parties will create too much unhappiness for you on a continual basis. If it will, the profession is not for you. Don't delude yourself, though. You will never find a profession or career that will have *everything* you want.

What weaknesses or dislikes are holding you back? What can you start working on? Now rank your weaknesses and dislikes in order.

If you have trouble identifying your strengths and weaknesses, you may want to enlist the help of someone who knows you well. If you do, be extremely careful that the person you choose will be totally objective. The last thing you need is for someone who is too close to you to tell you little white lies to make you feel better or avoid hurting your feelings.

Summary of Your Evaluation

1. List all your strengths: everything you feel that you are good at or have a talent for. Rank them in order.
2. List all the things you like to do.
3. List all your weaknesses: the traits that hold you back in life. Rank them in order.
4. List all the things you dislike.
5. What strengths can you make stronger? Do they work toward your ultimate dream?
6. What weaknesses can you eliminate? Which ones are holding you back from your dream? Do you need outside help?
7. After reviewing your strengths and weaknesses, do you feel your dream is attainable?
8. Put your plan away for several days.

Do What Needs To Be Done

Determination is the final consideration. Now that you know what it takes, are you willing to do what's necessary? It may take many years, a sacrifice of time from pleasurable activities for a while, a surrender of present finances and lifestyle. Your dream will not come easily. You must be prepared to go after it with all you've got. Don't look for, or depend upon, luck. Remember that luck requires you to be well-prepared when opportunity knocks.

Don't go on to Chapter 8, *Your Current Dilemma*, until you feel satisfied that you've done all the research necessary and made an honest evaluation of whether you have the right stuff to make your dream come true.

Figure 7.1 Sample Evaluation Checklist

Strengths and Weaknesses

List all your strengths and likes and all your weaknesses and dislikes under each category. Don't hold back!

Strengths and Likes

Personal:_____

_____

Social:_____

_____

Scholastic:_____

_____

Professional:_____

_____

Financial:_____

_____

Weaknesses and Dislikes

Personal:_____

_____

Social:_____

_____

Scholastic:_____

_____

Professional:_____

_____

Financial:_____

_____

8

Your Current Dilemma

Let's look at your current situation. You can't formulate a game plan without looking at what's going on in the real world. The dream world must wait a little longer. Have patience; you'll get there. At this point you should be thoroughly convinced that your dream is obtainable if you do what's needed.

Use a journal, spiral notebook, loose-leaf binder or legal pad. On the first page write your name, today's date and the time of day. Next write down the question, "Where am I?" and the statement, "This is where I am."

Don't write anything else for a while—just keep thinking about the question and the statement. Try to clear your mind of all your daily problems—such as earning a living, paying the rent or figuring out what you're going to eat next.

Try to get a clear picture in your mind—not the day-to-day stuff—but who you really are and how you got to where you are today. Reflect on all that is good and bad in your life. It's important that you get a firm grip on reality and how you got to this point in life.

Write down everything; you can reread and edit later. State everything exactly as it is today, not the way you would like it to be. Start with your career; it's probably the main reason you're unhappy now and feel handcuffed. List each item under the appropriate category as follows.

Professional

Prepare a complete resume of your career path. Start with the first job you ever held—even if it was part-time during your early teens—and continue through to your present position and job. (See Figures 8.1–8.3.) Include additional part-time jobs, moonlighting and civic or charity work. List all your skills even if they are only partial skills or skills you've learned informally or hands-on.

How did you get where you are today? Was it planned? If so, why do you feel trapped? Are you disillusioned with the field you're in, or is it just the company you presently work for? Maybe it's the people you work for or with. The reason for this exercise is to make sure that you are not about to throw away a good career that pays well just because you are currently unhappy. Don't do anything rash that you'll regret later. You've probably spent a lot of time getting where you are.

Did you get where you are by accident or as the result of a set of circumstances that derailed your original career plans? Were you pushed into your career by well-meaning family or friends? Are you bored, not challenged by what you spend so much time doing every day? Age and experience tend to change a person's outlook on life. Are you just going through mid-life crisis? Don't make a major change in your life just for the sake of change. Your dream should be something you really want, not just an escape from the present.

Another necessary reason for looking at how you got to where you are today is to ensure that you don't repeat mistakes. As George Santayana wrote, "Those who cannot remember the past are condemned to repeat it."

Figure 8.1   Scholastic Background

Describe your scholastic background listing all the schools you have attended, grades completed and any special courses or training you have taken. List any informal or on-the-job training. Are you proficient in more than one language?

_____

_____

_____

_____

_____

_____

_____

_____

_____

_____

_____

_____

_____

_____

Figure 8.2   Financial Background

Prepare a financial statement that includes the following information:

- Net income (after taxes)

    Yearly   _____

    Monthly   _____

- Savings

    Savings accounts   _____

    Stocks   _____

    IRAs   _____

    Etc.   _____

- Debts

    Mortgage   _____

    Loans   _____

    Credit cards   _____

    Etc.   _____

- Monthly expenses

    Housing
        Rent, mortgage payment _____

    Utilities
        Electric   _____

    Gas   _____

    Water   _____

    Phone   _____

    Food   _____

Figure 8.2   Financial Background (Cont'd)

- Monthly expenses (cont'd)

  Clothing   _____

  Transportation
    Automobile, bus   _____

    Train, cabs   _____

    Etc.   _____

  Insurance   _____

  Medical and dental   _____

  Entertainment   _____

  Vacations and travel   _____

  Etc. (I don't know where
  the money went!)   _____

Preparing an informal financial statement now will help you prepare your financial plan later. It will also help you identify where your money goes each month. To get a fast read on how you stand financially, add up your monthly expenses and compare the total with your monthly net income. How much do you have left each month? Are you able to save anything at this point? Begin to identify expenses that you could cut out to invest in pursuing your dream.

Figure 8.3   Personal Background

Appearance and Background Statistics.

Age_____   Hair Color_____   Eye Color_____

Sex_____   Complexion_____   Height_____

Weight_____   Bone Structure_____

Spouse_____   Race_____

Children_____   Grandchildren_____

Relatives_____   Family Structure_____

Religion_____   Family Background_____

Clothing.
Describe all your clothing and accessories as follows:

	Warm weather	Cold weather
Casual:	_____	_____
	_____	_____
	_____	_____
Sports:	_____	_____
	_____	_____
	_____	_____
Work:	_____	_____
	_____	_____
	_____	_____
Dress-up:	_____	_____
	_____	_____
	_____	_____

This inventory will be helpful when you begin to make your game plan and decide whether you need new clothing and how much it will cost.

Figure 8.3 Personal Background (Cont'd)

Health and lifestyle.
Describe your current state of health.

_____

_____

Describe your lifestyle: active, moderate or sedentary.

_____

_____

List your hobbies and sports/exercise activities.

_____

_____

Describe your eating habits and regular diet.

_____

_____

_____

Living conditions and standards.
Describe where you live, the kind of house or apartment you live in, and list your major possessions.

_____

_____

_____

_____

_____

_____

Figure 8.4   Social Background

Describe your social life and activities—personal, business and friendships.

_____

_____

_____

_____

_____

_____

_____

_____

_____

_____

The Control Factor

Mark an X next to everything you had or could have had some measure of control over.

How many things happened in your life that you had no control over? I don't mean the obvious things such as your parents and relatives, your birthplace, where and how you were raised, your genes, general health or early schooling. I mean things such as accidents, a health crisis, loss of a job or income due to factors you had no control over—or the loss of a relative or loved one.

How many things happened in your life that you had some measure of control over? These include things such as schools, courses, training, career, jobs, where and how you live, relationships and friendships, and current achievements, or lack of them.

Try not to concentrate on the things that you had no control over whatsoever. Start learning how to accept that life has, and always will have, uncertainties and events that will have some effect on you. These things will happen no matter what you do. There is no way that you can plan for them, avoid them or control them.

If you learn to accept the things in life that you cannot change, things you have no control over, then you start to relieve yourself of a major burden. Quit worrying about these things. On the other hand, if you can recognize the things you can change—the things you have some measure of control over—and start doing something to change them, you have started to change your life.

This exercise will help you to start focusing on the things in your life that you *do* have some control over. It won't give you a higher IQ, and it won't change your basic physical appearance. But it will change your outlook on life and start to give you the opportunity to plan and control a large part of your life. It will help you discover your natural resources and use them to their fullest. It will help you build the confidence in yourself that you need to pursue your dream.

After you've refined your list of things you had control or would have had control over, ask yourself these questions: Did I give thought or planning to these items? What things am I happy with? What things am I unhappy with? What do I want to keep? Hindsight is always better than foresight. Learn from your past; it's still your best reference material.

Breather #2

Put your current dilemma away for several days, and let the subconscious mind work on it. Now take another breather for a while. You could be feeling a bit low thinking that there is no hope. If you have done this step thoroughly and honestly, you have finished the hardest part.

Don't look at anything in your current dilemma for several days. Let your subconscious mind work on it for a while. After a few days' reflection, read over everything again and update your lists.

9

Making Your Game Plan

Consider your reserves. How long could you survive without your present job? Lower your lifestyle short-term. Cut out luxuries, and start downsizing. Put money away. Do you have access to credit? Can you get loans from friends or family? You can find a number of ways to save money. I'm an avid reader, and during my adjustment period I quit buying so many books and rediscovered the library. Look at your current lifestyle to see if there are ways to build a reserve.

How will your family react? What about your friends and business associates? Will they support you or disenfranchise you?

You've now determined exactly where you are in your current dilemma. You've identified your dream or where you want to be, determined that you have the right stuff and identified your strengths and weaknesses. Now you can begin to map out your game plan.

If all this work seems very difficult and time-consuming, it's a good sign that you really worked on it and completed it to the best of your ability. If you breezed through it and considered it a waste of time, you might want to go back over it. A good game plan requires a lot of hard work. You'll get out of it exactly what you put into it.

Threats and Opportunities

Always consider potential threats and opportunities. Obviously you won't be able to anticipate all of them, but it's important to spend time thinking through them very carefully.

A threat is anything that can have an adverse effect on your ability to achieve your dream. You may or may not have any control over potential threats. They can involve unforeseen financial or health situations, unanticipated changes in your career/professional or personal life or changes in laws that will have some effect on your long-range dream goal.

An opportunity is something that can help you achieve your dream. Opportunities can include financial help, changes in lifestyles or laws. An opportunity also can come in the form of a sudden increase of want, need or demand for what you have to offer. A good example is the recent opening of the Eastern European countries and a surge in the need for talented business people fluent in languages and customs of that area. If your background or talent can fulfill an aspect of this new need, you would be in a perfect position to offer your services. Always allow for the unforeseen events of both positive and negative natures. Keep your plan flexible enough so that you will not be thrown into a tailspin if a disaster hits or be unable to respond to a sudden opportunity if it arises. Keep your eye on your dream, but also keep your eye open to the outside world.

Start Your Game Plan

Where and when do you start? You've identified your dream. Treat it as a reality. Your dream is your ultimate destination. Your game plan will be a map of how to get there.

Your strategy is the logic through which you hope to achieve your dream. Try not to compare yourself to other people and their progress in life. You are unique. Try to build a healthy attitude, confident of what you want to do with your life. As you start building your personal game plan, try to start on a self-improvement program of proper diet, rest and exercise. Concentrate on eliminating or reducing bad habits at this time. Dedication, concentration and meditation will help you make a plan that will work for you and lead to a happier and fuller life.

Last-Minute Checklist

1. Do I now know what is needed, wanted or demanded by the dream I'm pursuing? In other words, do I know the requirements needed to achieve it?
2. Have I been honest in listing whether I have the right stuff—my strengths and weaknesses?
3. Have I been thorough in the research and analysis of my dream?
4. Am I absolutely certain at this point that my dream is the one I want and have a realistic chance of achieving?
5. How long will it take me to reach my goal? What are the short-range steps I need to take?

The Game Plan

Use a notebook to record your game plan. Use the checklist on the following page to help you get started, and follow the instructions for each area (see Figure 9.1). As always, take as much space as you need.

Figure 9.1   The Game Plan

Current Dilemma

Use this space to briefly recap your present status. This will serve as a reminder of where you are today.

_____

_____

Dream Goal

Write down your dream goal.

_____

_____

Short-Range Goals

All these goals should be directed toward helping you achieve your dream. You will probably have short-term goals in each of these five categories.

Personal:

• What attributes have you decided to work on, such as exercise or diet?

_____

_____

• What are the acceptable dress codes or expectations for your dream goal?

_____

_____

Social:

• What social goals will help you achieve your dream?

_____

_____

Figure 9.1   The Game Plan (Cont'd)

Scholastic:
- What schooling will be necessary?
- What other training will be necessary?

_____

_____

Professional:
- What are the short-range goals in your present job that will help you achieve your dream goal?

_____

_____

- What other jobs might you need to experience before achieving your dream goal?

_____

_____

- What on-the-job training will be necessary?

_____

_____

Financial:
- Where do you want to be financially in one, five or ten years? _____

_____

- What steps must be taken now to ensure that you can pursue your dream and not suffer severe financial setbacks? _____

_____

- Where can you obtain additional sources of financial aid if necessary?_____

_____

Figure 9.1   The Game Plan (Cont'd)

After you have listed your goals, make lists of the next areas. Keep updating them as situations occur. Refer to these lists often as you analyze and improve your plan in future months and years.

Strengths and Weaknesses

- Having noted your strengths, how can you improve them? _____

  _____

  _____

  _____

  _____

- What weaknesses or bad habits do you want to get rid of? Which ones are keeping you from achieving your dream? _____

  _____

  _____

  _____

  _____

- What are your goals for eliminating weaknesses and emphasizing strengths in each of the five categories? _____

  _____

  _____

  _____

  _____

Figure 9.1   The Game Plan (Cont'd)

Threats and Opportunities

- Do you know of any threats that may keep you from achieving your dream? Are there any opportunities that may arise that will help you achieve your dream? List them as you become aware of them.

Threats

_____

_____

_____

_____

_____

Opportunities

_____

_____

_____

_____

_____

Alertness toward the Unknown

Leave this space blank for now. If a disaster or setback blindsides you, take the time to write it down here for analysis as you update your plan.

_____

_____

_____

_____

Figure 9.1 The Game Plan (Cont'd)

Research

Make a list of all research that you need to do before you can achieve the goals in your game plan. Remember that research is usually nothing more than being alert—looking and listening to what is going on around you. Just because you have completed the initial research doesn't mean you should stop. Research should be an ongoing, daily exercise. Things change rapidly today, and you should keep your game plan current.

_____

_____

_____

_____

_____

Rest, Relaxation, Exercise

Make it a goal to allow time each week to recharge your batteries and let the subconscious mind work. List activities that you can make a routine each week. Pursuing your dream—while still working at a current job that's necessary to pay the bills—can wear you down and make you less productive. Be careful!

_____

_____

_____

_____

_____

10

Putting Your Plan into Action

An action plan means just that—ACTION! Now that you have clearly and realistically identified the things that must be done to make your dream come true, you must take action to make them start happening. An action plan identifies what you must do, where you must do it, when you must do it, how you must do it and how much it will cost in time as well as money.

Before you start working on this step, try the following technique of getting rid of unnecessary information.

Cutting Down the Weeds

Years ago I worked with someone in Ohio who taught me a valuable lesson. William was in charge of marketing for an advertising agency that handled my account. He would work long and hard on a client's marketing plan until he felt he could do no more. If he finished in the middle of the week or the middle of the night, it didn't matter. He would leave the office and disappear for two or three days on a mission that he would call *cutting down the weeds*. The first thing he would do was pack a bag, load up the car with sports gear and take off somewhere. It really didn't matter where. Sometimes he went fishing, camping and hiking; sometimes he went to a resort to play golf and tennis. He did this, he told me, to completely clear his mind of the marketing plan. He let it simmer for a while without any help from anyone. After recuperating from a vigorous physical sabbatical and a good night's sleep, William would return to his office and look at the plan again from a fresh viewpoint. He always said that when he returned to a plan after this short respite, it would be as if he'd never seen it before. He then started cutting away the weeds so that he could see the trees and the garden. In other words, he removed everything from the plan that was unnecessary and got in the way of seeing the ultimate goal or objective.

Nobody ever worried about William when he disappeared for a few days. They just said, "William's out cutting down the weeds." This technique worked very well for him; both he and his agency profited from it.

I've learned to use William's technique in my personal life. When my world seems muddled and overwhelming, I walk away from everything for a short period of time and do what I can to take my conscious mind off my current life. The subconscious keeps working—sometimes better—while the conscious takes a rest. After I've stopped long enough to feel refreshed, I start cutting down the weeds. I leave only the things I want; everything else is thrown out.

This technique works. It can be used for almost any problem in life that seems to overwhelm me. I now consider all the little daily and weekly chores that need to be done and errands that need to be run, as weeds in my mental garden. When they pile up and accumulate, they become worrisome irritants that distract. I've made it a habit to do them as they are necessary each day as quickly as possible. When I have to run an errand, I quickly think of how many things I can accomplish with that one trip.

As you work on your action plan, try to cut down the weeds and clear out everything that is unnecessary or getting in your way. Focus on the dream. Be persistent, diligent and committed.

Don't try to move into fifth gear right away. Ease into your action plan, and start to become comfortable with it. Increase your work on it gradually until you get up to speed. At that point, you will find what you are capable of and comfortable with on a daily/weekly basis. When you find the right pace, you may want to go back and change the completion dates on some of your goals. Be realistic, and don't try to achieve them overnight. Work in some time for relaxation and exercise. Pace yourself.

Getting started and staying with it become a long process. If you don't stay with it every day, like everything else, it will become something you think about or work on occasionally. You must try to work on your action plan as a daily habit, even if it's just to review your plan. Make copies of your plan, and take a copy with you. You don't have to become obsessive about it, but if you make it a daily routine, after a while you will work on your plan constantly without conscious thought.

Using the game plan you completed in the previous step, start working on your action plan (see Figure 10.1). The action plan consists of specific action programs of What, Where, When, How and Costs.

Write your long-range dream goal at the top of your action plan. If you have been diligent in your research and thoroughly understand your strengths and weaknesses, you will now have all the information you need and know all the requirements for achieving this goal.

What attributes did you decide were needed regarding your appearance? Plan your specific diet and exercise program, including what, where, when, how, time involved and costs. What does your wardrobe need, and how much will all of it cost?

What are the scholastic requirements to achieve your dream? Be specific in terms of certificates or degrees needed. Where will you go for these? When will you be able to start studies, and how will you fit your studies into your present schedule? Will your schooling require night and weekend study or a full-time program? How much total time will be required—six months, one year, two years? How much will all of this cost?

Is additional training necessary, such as courses on specific skills? Again, list what, where, when, how, how much time involved and what the costs are. Also include any additional needs, such as books or equipment.

Do you have opportunities in your present job or career that will help you achieve your dream? What are they, when can you start and how much time will be necessary?

Having noted your strengths, how can you improve them? What weaknesses or bad habits do you want to get rid of? Be specific.

Prepare a complete financial plan for budgeting purposes. Use the budget you prepared earlier in your current dilemma in which you listed your present income and financial resources and deducted all your living expenses. Now total all the costs involved in your action plan. Will you have the resources to finance your plan? If not, go over your budget in detail to find areas where you can make some sacrifices. Will you need to obtain outside financial help? If so, where, when and how? You may find it necessary to delay some of your short-range goals until you are able to afford them.

Your action plan should include everything necessary to achieve your dream. The components of the action plan become a series of short-range goals. Use a monthly

Figure 10.1 The Action Plan

*Long-range dream goal:*_____

Write down specific action programs to reach the goals outlined in the game plan. For each program, be sure to include what, where, when, how, how much time involved and what the costs will be:

Personal
  Physical   _____
                _____
                _____
  Clothing   _____
                _____
                _____
Social   _____
                _____
                _____
Scholastic
  Courses   _____
                _____
                _____
  Training   _____
                _____
                _____
Professional _____
                _____
                _____
Financial   _____
                _____
                _____

Figure 10.2   Threats and Opportunities

List the potential threats and opportunities that may affect your action plan.

Threats

_____

_____

_____

Opportunities

_____

_____

_____

---

calendar to schedule each of the activities required in your action plan. You should make a schedule for the entire year since some of your short-range goals require a certain number of weeks or months to complete. Don't forget to schedule time for family, rest and relaxation.

When you are finished, look over your monthly schedules to see if they are achievable. Are you too overloaded? Can you find gaps in some months that allow you to schedule other goals? Once you have mapped out the entire year, you can transfer the information to a pocket planner for ease of use and reference.

Review your action plan until you are absolutely positive it is achievable in terms of time and costs involved. When it's completed to your satisfaction, start putting it to work. Decide on a start date, and stop procrastinating.

Monitoring Your Progress

Controls are an essential part of your dream plan. They are nothing more than a means of monitoring your progress and revising your plan to incorporate more of what works and less of what doesn't work.

Daily/Weekly

Use your action plan on a daily basis to make sure that you are working on all your action programs. For the first month, it helps to keep a log of how much time it takes on a daily and weekly basis to complete all the segments of your programs. At the end of the first month, you will have a better idea of what you can accomplish on a daily and weekly basis without stretching yourself to the limit. It's important to be diligent in the pursuit of your ultimate dream. Trying to rush or cram too much into each day and week, however, will start to tire you out and will have an adverse effect on your overall plan. Remember that this program is designed for a lifetime.

Six Months

Try to set aside a weekend all by yourself. Take your action plan and review it. What areas of the plan don't seem to be working? Why aren't they working? Can you correct them?

Don't rewrite your plan, but evaluate your progress and cross out items that you have not been able to work on during the past six months. If you have not found time to work on them, you are stretching yourself too far. Put these items back in at a later date when you feel that you can set aside time to work on them and finish them.

Did anything happen in the past six months to help or hinder your progress on the plan? Did you have any control over these events? If not, don't beat yourself up. If you had control and didn't exercise it, again, don't beat yourself up. Learn from the mistake, and don't repeat it. You have made excellent progress because you are in control of knowing what happened and have the ability to take steps to correct any mistakes you make. Your action plan is a map to lead the way. If you make a little detour occasionally, that's okay. At least you have a map to guide you back.

Year-End Review

Make a *new* plan for next year starting from the beginning. Even if your dream goal, supporting goals and other goals are the same, it's beneficial to rewrite your plan each year to help you keep a sharp focus on your progress. You will also find that your current dilemma will be different from last year with progress in many areas, and you will want to add or delete parts of your action programs.

If you are not making the kind of progress you had planned on a year ago, review all aspects of your game plan and action plan to find areas where you haven't progressed. Isolate these items, and make part of next year's plan a concentrated effort to correct them. You may even want to re-evaluate your dream goal. It's time to ask yourself if it's something that you still want or are capable of achieving. If it's not, don't become disenchanted or think that you have wasted a year. You have learned new disciplines and are still in charge of your life. You are ahead of the average person because you are consciously trying to map out your life and free yourself from corporate bondage. Making a wrong turn or a detour occasionally is not a disaster.

If you have been diligent in following and monitoring your game plan and your action plan, you now have a pretty good record of what you did the previous year and have the ability to isolate the problems and correct them. Many people just look back on last year, say, "What happened?" and crash right into the next year. They make the same mistakes over and over again and become even more trapped.

If you are happy with your progress, *don't* lay back and become lazy in the new year. Make a new plan, and use it to improve upon your new strengths and progress. Eliminate or *cut down the weeds* around all the things you don't need from last year's plan. The key to success is to avoid complacency and to continue to improve year after year. Some people always say, "If it works, don't fix it." This saying does not apply to making your dream happen. If it works, find out *why* and make it better. Keep improving upon it. The key here is knowing *why* it works. Your plan will be a constant companion for life, helping you control rather than be controlled.

The main reason you should prepare a new plan every year is that the wants, needs and demands of your dream may constantly change. Your yearly plan will keep you focused on these changes and keep you on the right track.

Feedback

Use another person to analyze your plan—someone you admire, respect and trust. If you choose to have someone else review your dream plan, be sure to select someone who will review the plan with total objectivity. That person must be brutally honest in the evaluation of your plan, you as a person and your capabilities.

Test Marketing

As you try out new strategies, learn to observe how they are received. Listen to what other people say. Use this information to strengthen the strategies that work, and discard the ones that don't work.

Make a habit of keeping a copy of your action plan with you at all times. Review your goals daily, review your performance and see if your behavior matches your goals.

12

The Great
Escape

When will the big day come? When can you escape
from corporate bondage and throw those golden handcuffs away forever? Unless you're extremely lucky, the
handcuffs won't disappear that quickly. You can't pull a
Houdini here. Those who have made their dreams come
true will tell you that it took time, effort and most
importantly, a strong determination to stay with it. There
will be times when you want to give up—days when you
feel like a dismal failure and get angry with yourself for
even daring to think you could succeed. *Don't give up!*

Maybe you can't break the handcuffs right away, but
you can sure loosen them a bit. Consider the Chinese
proverb—"The journey of a thousand miles begins with a
single step." Once you take that first step, you're well on
your way to the great escape. The first step is the hardest.
Once you've taken it, celebrate. Be proud of yourself.

I realized that it could take ten or more years for me to reach my ultimate dream—to become a full-time writer. My first step was deciding to do it, but I made my journey easier by leaving the corporate world and opening my own business. I found a way to accomplish my ultimate dream. I've always dreamt of achieving independence, and I've succeeded. I've never been happier.

My final escape from corporate bondage is still more than three years away, but I consider my decision to pursue my dream to be my *great escape*. You may find a way to plateau your journey as well. Many others have.

Although ten years may sound like a long time, it really isn't. Many of my students become discouraged when they first start making a game plan. They feel that they can't wait one more day to live their dreams once they've decided to pursue them. They want success now! I have one answer: Those people who are unwilling to invest time and effort into achieving their dreams probably won't succeed.

Your dream might not require ten years. If your dream is writing, be forewarned—ten years may be an optimistic timeline. Many successful writers have spent much longer trying to make their dreams come true. One thing that successful writers have in common is their determination. They find the time to write while supporting themselves and their families with day jobs. Some get up early and write for several hours before they go to work. Others wait until the family goes to bed and write far into the night. The key is that they carve out time to write every day.

Most dreams in the artistic fields will require you to support yourself with jobs that you don't particularly like. This is reality. If you want your dream badly enough, you'll find a way to make it happen. A few lucky ones may have a family, spouse or an *angel* to support them while they pursue their dream full-time.

If your dream is to open a small business, your time-table will probably be much shorter. Factors such as getting the proper training or raising capital are the only barriers. Even if you are able to start your business in a short period of time, however, it may take you many years to make it successful. But the handcuffs will be gone; you'll be living your dream.

If your dream is to become a doctor, dentist, scientist, lawyer or other professional, the time and money for school will be the determining factors for how long it will take you to succeed.

There is no way I can tell you how long it will take to make your dream come true or to escape corporate bondage. Every person has a slightly different dream, different circumstances to contend with and different degrees of skill and training. You will have to determine your own timing. My hope is that this book will help you decide what's needed to proceed and motivate you to get busy with your game plan. The sooner you start, the sooner you'll break free.

Part 3

Those Who Did It— How They Did It

This book is not classroom theory. All the steps have been field-tested time and again—by myself and by the people I've profiled in this section.

Each account is one of hope and inspiration for all of us. The hardest part of finishing this book was deciding which stories to include. My list of people to interview grew daily; all their profiles would have filled volumes. The stories I have selected illustrate men and women from a variety of fields.

I would also like to state that I am not anti-corporate. I think, for the most part, that large corporations lost their way during the 1980s. Too much emphasis was put on profit and not on people. That will change in the future. Happy people are both loyal and productive—they make companies grow. The people who are leaving large companies are the new pioneers. They know firsthand what caused the downfall of many major American corporations. They will take us back to the roots of our country's growth. The trend is already there: The U.S. Bureau of Labor Statistics shows that small businesses now account for 40 percent of the gross national product and most of the jobs created since 1980.

Every large company in the world today started out as one person's dream.

Pamela Call, M.D. : Photo by Michael Dainard

13

She's On Call Now

Pamela Call, M.D.

Pamela Call became a practicing psychiatrist in 1988 at the age of 45. She is now 49 and has her offices on Fifth Avenue in New York City. That's quite an achievement when you consider that it takes nine years to become a doctor—four years of medical school, four years in internship and residency training and a one-year fellowship. That's an exhausting schedule for someone in their early 20s just graduating from college. Pamela was in her mid-30s when she made the decision to go to medical school, and she was still two credits short of a college degree.

Needless to say, Dr. Call received more than a little criticism about her decision to change careers. She was well-respected in the world of fashion. Ben Shaw, a major backer in the fashion industry, had just offered to start a new company on Seventh Avenue and let Pamela run it

for him. Shaw is well known for the many famous designers he has brought under his umbrella companies—
including designers Bill Blass, Halston, Geoffrey Beene
and Oscar de la Renta. Pamela Call was not turning her
back on a minor career.

Deciding to do it was the easy part. Making it happen
was to become a major life achievement. To start with,
how could she even hope to find a medical school that
would accept a woman in her mid-30s with a fashion and
drama background who was two credits short of a college
degree? Sheer and utter madness, most friends told her.
Medical schools had the choice of the lot from many, many
applicants more qualified and younger than she was.
Pamela applied to 48 schools before she was finally
accepted. Most people would have given up after the first
dozen. But Pamela kept at it and made her dream come
true.

Pamela Ullman (Call) was born in 1943 in Crystal
Falls, Michigan, the only child of a 65-year-old father and
30-year-old mother. Pamela's father was the owner of
several lumber mills; her mother stayed at home with her.
Pamela was adored and doted on. She spoke full sentences
by the time she was six months old but didn't walk until
she was two. Pamela compares her early life to the
infamous little princess joke, "She can walk...but why
should she have to?"

When Pamela was six, her life changed dramatically.
Her father lost his business, and the family had to move
to a small town in northern Minnesota. When she was
nine, Pamela's father was killed in a tragic accident, and
her mother went to work as a secretary. Their lifestyle
had dropped to what Pamela described as "poor." She
didn't really have a sense of this in a town with one
restaurant and a gas station. Status differences were not
so clear. Pamela had a job to do, going to school, and she
took it very seriously.

At the age of ten, the first *accidental* push of Pamela's early career move happened. Her music class was part of a statewide competition, and Pamela was selected from more than 5,000 students to become the 1953 singing Christmas Seal child. She traveled throughout the state performing and later was asked to sing in many concerts, benefits and community gatherings. Loving the attention, Pamela began to turn her aspirations to becoming a performer.

In high school, Pamela excelled in public speaking, acting and performing. In the routine career counseling given by her school, she hardly considered career choices other than these three areas, and she won a scholarship to a prestigious university theater program. Looking back, Pamela feels it was ironic that the courses she excelled in and enjoyed the most were in the sciences—biology, chemistry and physics. Her teachers tried unsuccessfully to fan her interest in choosing one of these areas as a career path.

Pamela graduated from high school in 1961, second in her class. Her best friend was first in the class and had chosen to become a doctor. Pamela recalls envying her friend's choice and thinking how interesting the study of medicine would be. Pamela's one area of miserable academic performance, however, was math. Her friend was a math whiz, and Pamela felt she could never catch up. Besides, her friend had picked medicine first.

Pamela's efforts at the university were rewarded with much success. She was cast often and spent most of her time rehearsing and performing in the theater group. This became a detriment to her other academic courses, but she just didn't care—an actress didn't need freshman English. In spite of her efforts and energy in the arts, she made straight As in biology. Two credits short of a bachelors degree, she left the university.

Pamela leaped into professional theater, spending three years as a technician and an actress in repertory theater. During this time she met her future husband, Edward Call, a theatrical director. His life demanded that he travel from theater to theater, so Pamela traveled with him. She began to realize that she didn't have the kind of commitment or deep love to continue on this career path where even the most talented spent 80 percent of their time looking for work and 20 percent working. Pamela gave up her pursuits, in retrospect, with very little thought or regret. This dream was not for her.

Pamela's talented husband was the artistic director for a major theater, and the Calls enjoyed considerable social visibility. Pamela directed her efforts toward being a housewife and helping Edward entertain. Occasionally she would amuse herself by taking modeling assignments. It became more than an amusement when they moved to New York, however, and Edward's career took a downturn. Modeling then became work to help support the couple.

Even from the beginning, Pamela was less than enthusiastic about being a model. In theater, she was unable to tolerate the inconsistency and lack of schedule, and in modeling, the *go sees* became dreary, discouraging and painful. Eventually she landed a full-time job as a house model for a fashionable Fifth Avenue store. After several months, a well-known designer whose clothes Pamela had shown, courted her to his showroom. She was now *in the industry*. She became the designer's personal fitting model. During her three years working with him, she became his *right-hand everything* and moved into other areas of the company as director of public relations.

Pamela and the designer traveled extensively, had a celebrity clientele and designed clothes for Broadway and Hollywood. Her life was fast-paced, glamorous and exciting. But extravagant spending, poor business management and a shifting economy caused the designer's principal *angel* to pull the backing, and the business folded.

Pamela joined another talented designer with a growing business, but the atmosphere was more routine and bottom-line oriented. It was pleasant but definitely *no frills*. For the first time, she found herself in the real world of business on Seventh Avenue—her corporate bondage.

Pamela initially went into therapy to focus on the problems of dealing with a husband who had to be out of town ten months a year and of trying to adjust to life in New York City. It became clear that she was not finding much satisfaction in her work, which had now become her life focus. Questions began to arise about her goals and *fit* with her profession. Pamela had little in common with most of her colleagues and realized that she had few real friends in the business.

When her therapist started her on an exhaustive career counseling evaluation, Pamela expected that her strengths in the arts and public relations would emerge as the primary goal. Surprisingly, both interest and aptitude tests revealed major strengths in science, logical process activities and education. Pamela tested high in physics and language skills but low in self-confidence. The tests specifically showed that she should go back to school and pursue a field of science related to people. At 36, with an already established lucrative career, how could Pamela go back to school and still support herself?

The combination of extensive therapy and career counseling helped Pamela gain the self-confidence she needed to make a decision about her future. She wanted to become a physician. Nothing else interested her as much. Her marriage had, for all purposes, ended. She did not feel that she fit into the fashion industry even though she was successful in it. She had succeeded in a career she really didn't want or like. She felt that she shared nothing in common with her colleagues, but most of all, she felt that she was not doing anything worthwhile. Pamela felt a deep need to contribute—to feel that she was making a difference in the world. She needed to be involved in meaningful, satisfying work that amounted to more than just filling her (and other people's) pockets with money. That was her dream, and she decided to break her corporate bondage. Money and fame were no longer her goals.

First, Pamela needed the two credits to complete college. While working full-time at what she now considered her *day* job, she attended Hunter College and Fordham University, completing almost another full degree in psychology with a 4.0 average. She also liked the hard sciences and finally mastered her problem with math. Pamela had the right stuff to pursue her goal of becoming a doctor, now her definite life goal.

What surprised Pamela more than anything else was that many of her acquaintances and friends offered very little support in her new goal. She was discouraged by many about pursuing a medical degree and becoming a doctor. She was a model, an actress, a public relations director, a businesswoman—but surely not a doctor. When they couldn't dissuade her from her goal, many people told Pamela that if she still had her sights set on the medical field, she should at least lower them a little, to a more realistic goal—a "paraprofession"—a physician's assistant, perhaps, or a speech therapist. Pamela felt that these people were scoffing at the fact that a model could become a doctor. Most of them just couldn't understand why she would want to leave a profession she was successful in. Pamela was being courted for bigger and better jobs, more prestige, higher salaries, lucrative benefits and finally with the opportunity to run her own company. And she was turning her back on all of this—was she crazy or what?

The paperwork alone for applying to 48 medical schools is a career unto itself. The rejections were numbing in their frequency and abundance. Because of her background and age, most schools didn't consider Pamela to be a good risk. She was an interesting but *chancy* candidate. She kept at it, and finally she was accepted by New York

Medical College in 1978. Pamela financed her education with loans and help from friends. It wasn't easy, and her lifestyle changed dramatically.

Medical school is hard if you're in your early 20s and still used to regular study habits. It's even tougher as a *nontraditional* student. The courses are grueling, and your fellow students are 15 years younger. They have more stamina. Pamela existed on an average of four or five hours' sleep a night. She graduated in 1983 at the top of her class—a member of Alpha Omega Alpha, the medical school honor society. She was 40 years old.

The next four years were not any easier as Pamela trained at one of New York's busiest hospitals, St. Vincent's in Greenwich Village. She was chief resident of the psychiatry program in her senior year. Her first real job was running and supervising the very busy psychiatric emergency room at the hospital. This job would not likely have been given to a person with less maturity. Next, Pamela earned a one-year fellowship at Memorial Sloan Kettering Cancer Center.

Nine years may seem like a long time to achieve your goal, but nine years of being unhappy almost every day can seem even longer. Deciding to do something about it— and then doing it—makes all the difference. In looking back, Pamela feels like it happened almost overnight. She was too busy doing what she loved to stop and think about how long it was taking. To her, the journey was as pleasurable as the destination.

Today Dr. Pamela Call is becoming one of New York's most respected psychiatrists, working with patients who have medical illnesses—cancer, AIDS, heart disease and trauma. Many of her patients are terminally ill, and she applies her skills in providing comfort, support and medicine to ease their suffering. Just prior to this interview, she was in Italy on a teaching assignment. Last year she traveled to China to provide AIDS education.

Pamela's days are full and satisfying. When she was in the fashion and theater business, she worked hard to go the extra mile, but the hard work was not satisfying. She needed to apply her energy to something that made a difference. She now gets up at 5:30 AM each day and makes early rounds at St. Vincent's. Her days are spent teaching as an assistant professor at New York Medical College and juggling private patients and referrals from other doctors. She's constantly being paged to attend to emergency surgery cases. Early evenings find her making the rounds at the hospital, then going back to her office to complete paperwork. It's not unusual for her to attend to several patients by phone late at night or see patients who are dying at home. Often Pamela's working days end close to midnight. Saturdays and Sundays are more of the same. What little free time Pamela has left is spent reading and studying medical journals. In fact most of this interview with her involved a succession of quick sandwiches grabbed in coffee shops in Greenwich Village.

Pamela has never worked so hard in her life, and she loves it. It shows! She's 49, looks 35 and says she feels like she's 20. Her early career path was set by many different circumstances, certainly not one that was planned. She too had become one of the successfully unhappy, but she decided to do something about it. Pamela Call, M.D., broke her corporate bondage and achieved her final reward, her dream come true.

LaVaun S. Eustice: Photo by Michael Dainard

14

Building a Boutique

LaVaun S. Eustice

LaVaun S. Eustice was my boss at New York University for more than five years as the assistant director of the Management Institute. Her responsibilities included development of the institute's programs; course design; curriculum evaluation; faculty selection; student advisement and school administration. She managed more than 250 courses annually and more than 100 faculty members. As we were discussing my new course, *Breaking the Golden Handcuffs*, she announced that she was resigning from NYU and breaking her own corporate bondage.

I was shocked. LaVaun had read the first draft of the manuscript for this book and decided that the time was right for her. This was no minor decision. LaVaun held a very senior executive position with one of the country's largest most prestigious universities. She was 58 years old and was giving up a lucrative career that would hold further advancement as well as a comfortable retirement in the near future.

With mixed emotions, I decided to interview her for this book. I was very happy for her, but selfishly, I will miss her very much. Four years ago LaVaun allowed me to break away from teaching my regular marketing courses and design my own courses. My other course, *Marketing Yourself*, had actually started the process for her. She said that she had read my last book and had been working on her personal marketing plan for some time. She had thought about making a change for more than a year. A major life change—and working on the design of my new course—became the nudge she needed to get serious.

LaVaun's last day at NYU was August 28, 1992. Her golden handcuffs are gone. In September she returned to school at Fashion Institute of Technology (FIT) to take courses in fashion buying and merchandising. It will take her 18 months to complete the courses. LaVaun's dream is to own a boutique emporium in a resort area, and her seasonal home will be above the shop. She plans on living half of her time in New York and half at the resort. It will be a very special and different kind of store, combining resort fashion wear, jewelry, accessories, scents, giftware, commissioned pieces and paper goods.

LaVaun envisions her shop having a living room atmosphere that is inviting and friendly. She plans to include a round table with chairs all around, fashion magazines to leaf through and coffee. Her customers will become her friends, not just tourists with money to spend. She will do all the buying for the shop—that's the other part of her dream. LaVaun loves to travel. She loves to meet new people. Her buying trips will allow her to do both. LaVaun's goal is not to make a lot of money; that's not her major concern. She wants to have fun and meet people. She wants to bring some style to resort wear. Most of the shops in resort areas are stocked with some pretty awful, boring stuff.

LaVaun has all the right stuff to make her dream come true, but while working on her plan, she realized that she needed the training to become a professional buyer. So she decided that 18 more months of schooling were well worth the time, effort and expense. She wants to be well-prepared when she opens her boutique. Her savings and severance pay would help finance the transition. Her previous work experience includes jobs in marketing, advertising, special events, promotion and retailing. During her 18 months of school, LaVaun will also take courses in real estate, law, taxes, import and export, making a business plan and small business financing. She also has to decide which resort area to open in and choose a site location. So far LaVaun has done a lot of research on schools and courses, read a number of books and visited and interviewed shop owners in several resort areas. Next year LaVaun will start visiting different resort areas to determine where she wants to be. This is doubly important since she plans to live there part of the year. LaVaun has made a full assessment of what she needs to do to make her dream happen. There are no gaps.

Has LaVaun received a lot of criticism of her decision? You bet she did, mostly from colleagues and a few of her friends. They couldn't believe that she would quit a successful career to start a new one—especially at the age of 58, when most academic professionals are dreaming of retirement. Many of her close friends—and her daughter and son—are happy for her. Her family was surprised and wanted to know how she had ever thought of such a wonderful idea. Her 25-year-old daughter said, "Oh Mom, you are so *cool!*" LaVaun has all the support she needs, and she believes in herself. She will succeed just as she has in her other career paths.

At first LaVaun thought people would laugh at her, that she was just reacting to some life problems she was experiencing at the time or that this was some *silly female folly*. LaVaun talked with her therapist who told her that she had always succeeded at whatever she had done. LaVaun agreed, and this time she was doing it for herself. "I'll probably end up doing a lot of the same stuff," she said, " but now it'll be my priorities, and I won't have to deal with the internal politics that all large companies suffer from."

LaVaun was born in Park Ridge, Illinois, a suburb of Chicago. She has one sister, who is six years older than she is. Her father was an advertising executive, and her mother stayed at home until LaVaun and her sister were grown. Because of her father's profession, the family moved around quite a bit. When LaVaun started grade school, she lived in Pennfield, Pennsylvania. The family then moved to Cranford, New Jersey. When LaVaun was in the sixth grade, the family moved to a small town in Michigan, then back to Park Ridge where she attended high school.

In high school LaVaun's interest was journalism, so she worked on the school newspaper. In college she continued her journalism pursuit with the college newspaper and also concentrated on advertising. She graduated from the University of Illinois with a bachelor of science degree cum laude with university honors. She was elected to Phi Kappa Phi; Kappa Tau Alpha (communications); and Theta Sigma Phi (journalism).

LaVaun's first job was as a copywriter for Sears in their Chicago home office. She advanced to senior copywriter and worked for Sears for 11 years. When her two children came along, she stayed home for the next ten years. LaVaun kept her journalism skills current by designing the layout and writing the newspapers for her children's school.

When LaVaun decided to return to work after ten years, she needed to learn new skills, including how to use an electric typewriter and a copy machine. This was the start of her second career. In 1979 she landed a job as an office manager with the New York University Dental

Center. She assisted in managing and marketing programs, faculty/patient recruitment and ADA accreditation. During this time, she also created and wrote the office policy and procedures training manual. In less than two years, LaVaun was acting assistant director and promoted and managed more than 100 technical courses, conferences and clinics for dentists, auxiliaries and allied health professionals.

Two years of this was enough for LaVaun. She had returned to the workplace but became bored and felt the job was a dead end. Not wanting to just *work*, LaVaun needed a challenge and decided to switch careers again. She went back to school at The New School for Social Research, Graduate School of Management in New York. She received a master of professional studies degree with distinction, concentrating on tourism, travel and travel management. The recipient of the 1983-1984 outstanding graduate Tourism Award, LaVaun wrote her master's thesis on, "A Study of a Special Kind of Meetings Market: Continuing Professional Education."

In 1984, LaVaun went to work as a marketing coordinator for *Meetings & Conventions* magazine. For two years she assisted in special event management, client liaison and program evaluation. She also initiated analysis of the magazine's competition. In 1986 she was promoted to special events director, where she was responsible for all marketing support activities, including special events, trade shows, client-advertiser promotions in the hospitality industry and publication sales meetings.

LaVaun is not only a tireless worker; she is creative. She completely designed, negotiated and staged six annual domestic and international destination-inspection programs for qualified Fortune 500 company buyers. The programs she initiated included product sampling, educational seminars and VIP activities. LaVaun significantly increased awareness of the magazine by managing a series of golf tournaments, culminating in a championship play-off at Turnberry, Scotland, and orchestrating the awards banquet at the Waldorf Astoria in New York. LaVaun traveled extensively for the magazine, and here her love of travel began to grow.

In 1987, Rupert Murdoch's *News America* bought *Meetings & Conventions* magazine and decided to move the offices to New Jersey. LaVaun didn't want to commute, so she left the magazine. She was teaching a course at NYU, *Meetings and Conference Management*, and took a full-time job with the Management Institute.

LaVaun flourished as the assistant director. The part of her job she liked the best was the creative end, looking for needs in the school and designing new courses. The part she hated was the administrative end, and as this became more and more of her responsibility, she derived less and less satisfaction from her work.

What pushed LaVaun over the line was a life change. A little more than three years ago, she developed a persistent cough, and the diagnosis was lung cancer. LaVaun continued working through her treatment— chemotherapy and daily radiation treatments. The treatments are worse than most diseases. She went through the usual partial hair loss, suffered through nausea and debilitating fatigue. Most people never knew she was sick. Her strong will, positive attitude and a healthy constitution helped her beat the disease, and she continues to test negative.

LaVaun's children are grown and out of the nest, and she is in the process of divorce. As she looked around, LaVaun saw that the major portion of her life revolved around her career. She felt that she now had to do something that she *really* wanted to do—something just for herself. She wasn't sure what that was. Her entire career had been as an employee, working for someone else. When her marriage was intact and her children still at home, work was just a part of LaVaun's life. Now it *was* her life. As she worked on her personal marketing plan,

LaVaun listed what she liked to do best: She likes to shop; she loves to travel; she likes being creative and organizing things; she likes people.

LaVaun is excited about traveling with a new sense of purpose, to seek out new and exciting merchandise for her shop. She expects to meet many new friends in her travels, including the craftspeople from whom she will commission works. She knows she will love running the store too. As a teenager she worked in a bake shop and loved it, especially the interaction with customers.

I asked LaVaun what suggestions she might have for others who are considering making a break. Her advice is to take some courses on the subject of the career they are considering. Do a lot of research; talk to people, read a lot of books on the subject. Most importantly, face the reality of your abilities. "I absolutely love art, but I would never consider opening an art gallery," she said. "I don't have that *inborn knowledge* necessary to discover new artists who will be the new wave."

LaVaun's new boutique emporium will be her living room. She expects people to keep coming back to poke around, chat over coffee and look over new merchandise. One of the major differences she plans is that she will constantly be changing the look of the shop, that new merchandise will be arriving every week to keep a fresh and exciting look. It will become a destination for customers, not just a place to shop if it's raining or they're bored.

Is she scared? "I'm terribly excited right now." LaVaun thought for a moment. "Once I made the decision to do it, a sense of relief flooded through me. I feel so alive...younger. I'll probably be scared when I locate my shop and sign a lease, but this is my sixth career change. I've never failed at anything I set my mind to doing."

Kathleen M. Giordano: Photo by Michael Dainard

15

Lady Barber

Kathleen M. Giordano

For a reasonable fee, the *Lady Barber* will come to your office to give you a haircut that fits your psyche, style, personality and physical characteristics. You save time because she comes to you. She sees you in your environment, your power base, your cave. The cut she gives you is just right! She also gives you valuable insight on your wardrobe and demeanor. She entertains you, makes you laugh and feel good about yourself. Kathleen is *not* a hairstylist; she is a barber. She cuts *only* men's hair, and she is always booked.

Irish-Italian Kathleen M. Giordano was born into a family of barbers in Havertown, Pennsylvania. She has five brothers and two sisters. Her father owns Penn Campus Barber Shop on the University of Pennsylvania campus where he employs three of her brothers, one of whom is her twin. Kathleen's first job was sweeping the floor in her father's shop when she was 12.

As far back as she can remember, Kathleen had a fascination with dolls and their hair. She'd cut it, style it and color it with magic markers. She loved to place all her dolls in a circle and entertain them, pretending to be both their mother and teacher. Kathleen played with dolls until she was in the ninth grade.

As a teenager, Kathleen worked nights in her father's shop learning to cut men's hair. Even though she loved barbering, it never occurred to her to pursue it as a profession. Both of her parents were adamant about her attending college and pursuing a career in the world of business. There were enough barbers in the family.

In high school, Kathleen was considered very creative. Her project for *World Culture* class was to pick a country and report on it. She made an attaché case and played the role of a detective traveling the continent. She graduated from Cardinal O'Hara High School in 1975, then went on to the Keystone School of Business where she received an associate degree. While attending Keystone, one of her favorite classes was *Public Speaking*. Her bubbly, expressive personality earned her straight As, and her professor considered her extremely talented. She began to think about pursuing a part-time acting career or modeling career in Philadelphia.

After business school, Kathleen went to work at the University of Pennsylvania Hospital in the radiology department as a medical secretary. She still wanted to be a model or an actress. One day she was flipping through a glamour magazine and saw a picture of a top model. She said to herself, "I can do this, I *want* to go to New York and live." At her meeting with the legal coordinator in the radiology department, she was just at the point of signing on the dotted line when she looked up and said, "I can't. I have to go to New York." Stunned, the coordinator told her that most people would cut off their right arms for the opportunity she was giving up. Kathleen put down the pen and walked out of the office.

That night at the dinner table she told her family. All hell broke loose. At first they didn't believe her and accused her of just wanting to move away to "have fun." In an Italian household, women were expected to move out of the house only when they got married. Determined, Kathleen secured an apartment through a roommate service. With only $1,000 to her name, no job to go to and no friends there, Kathleen moved to New York. Her parents were very angry with her at first, and her father said, "Give her six months, and she will be back home." That was 11 years ago. She's never regretted her decision.

Trying to become a model in New York is tough work, and Kathleen was scared. Her first roommate was neurotic and offered no support. Kathleen pounded on every agent's door in the city. Within three months, she was almost broke, but she was definitely not going to run back home. In desperation she took a job as a legal secretary working nights from 4:30 PM to 11 PM. During the day, she continued her relentless search to build a career as a model.

Two years went by. Kathleen was becoming discouraged, but she believed in herself and was determined that she would "make it." The friends she had made in New York all told her she would have better luck in Europe, that she had that *European look*. Besides, she could be groomed there and return to New York better equipped. As easy as this was to say, it was harder to do. Kathleen was then 27 years old. Most models go to Europe at 17, even 14; how could she expect to compete?

Finally, Kathleen met an Italian agent and lied through her teeth about her age. She got the job and became successful. She lived and modeled in Milan, Munich, Madrid, Zurich and Brussels. She modeled for catalogs, magazines, television and fashion shows, and graced the covers of magazines in Italy and Germany. After three years, Kathleen was all set to move to Vienna, then Paris, but she was burnt out. She just couldn't move to one more city, make the rounds and live among other models.

Kathleen loved Europe. She felt it was a sophisticated, growing experience, but modeling had taken its toll on her. Suffering from bulimia to keep thin and glamorous, Kathleen became insecure, and she was forced to question herself about her age, her life and what she really wanted to do.

Dejected and feeling aimless about her future, Kathleen returned to New York. She got her old job back as a legal secretary to support herself and started making the go-sees for modeling jobs. Kathleen got assignments, but her heart wasn't in modeling any more. She had done TV commercials while in Europe and was also trying to make a break into television as an actress.

But she still loved cutting men's hair. While on jobs in Europe, she had cut the male models' hair. She now thought about getting a barber's license, but a year went by before she decided to do it. Barbering was her first love, and it was time for her to become focused on her future. She started at the Atlas Barbering School in Manhattan. She needed 1,000 hours—about six months full-time. Her work schedule allowed her to attend only part-time, but she was able to complete the program in 13 months.

Kathleen apprenticed and went on to work for an exclusive salon in the Wall Street area. Her business background served her dramatically well, and in addition to cutting hair, she became manager and PR director. After 18 months, she became a New York State Master Barber, a license that allowed her to open her own place of business.

Kathleen had all the right stuff to become successful in business. She had proven herself as a model and was on the way to becoming an actress. No doubt her determination would have made her successful. Kathleen put her acting career on the back burner while she concentrated on building her clientele, but she still takes acting classes one night a week. She wants to cut men's hair. It's what makes her happy. Kathleen didn't like working in a salon for someone else; she wanted to become her own boss. She didn't have enough money to start her own shop and wouldn't dare ask her family for help. Kathleen broke her corporate bondage—her salary and security—and went out on her own to an inventive new venture.

Kathleen's corporate bondage involved working at something she didn't like. She had overcome tremendous odds to become a successful model in Europe. She was a whiz at business and could have returned to Wharton and become an executive with a major firm. Then, although working at something she loved—at a salon cutting men's hair—she hated being tied down and being told what to do. Kathleen is a free spirit. She needed to fly, and fly she did. Her business is one of the most innovative I've seen.

One Friday night, Kathleen quit her job. On Monday she took out her appointment book and called all her regular clients. She thanked them all for their past patronage and let them know she was going out on her own. She didn't try to raid her bosses' clientele—a few clients followed, and she built a small base.

It wasn't easy in the beginning. She came up with the name Lady Barber and designed a logo that she is in the process of trademarking. Next she printed up flyers explaining her *in office* service. Dressed in a business suit, she handed the flyers out on street corners near office buildings. Kathleen didn't like the way men looked at her and soon gave it up. Also, it broke her heart to see her flyers discarded in trash cans and gutters. Instead, she asked clients and friends for referrals. She started canvassing offices, leaving flyers with the receptionists and telling them what she was all about. Slowly her business started to build.

Drawing on her modeling experience of go-sees, Kathleen started pestering editors of newspapers and magazines. Creative and charged with pure energy, her efforts started paying off. Kathleen has been featured in numerous newspapers, magazines and television talk shows. Successful now, she never slows down. One Saturday before Memorial Day, she did 25 haircuts. By the end of the day, although exhausted, she felt like a million dollars. With Kathleen's energy and drive, she'll be worth a million some day. Count on it.

Kathleen has returned to her heritage and her first love—cutting men's hair. She's done it her way, with no salon, no boss and the freedom to choose her clients—mostly powerful and exciting executives. Kathleen's experience as a model has helped her. She shows up at a client's office in a business suit carrying an attaché case with the tools of her trade. If the client is a regular, she gets right to work. She knows the importance of time; she's a professional herself. On a first visit, Kathleen takes time to evaluate new clients. With a critical eye, she assesses the way their office looks, the way they dress, even their bone structure and features. Her engaging personality immediately draws them into telling her all about themselves.

One of Kathleen's biggest assets is that she builds strong relationships with her clients. She feels that they are an important part of her life, and she shows a genuine concern for them and their lives. She listens to what they say and earns their absolute trust. Sometimes she feels like she's their psychiatrist. After a period of time she's able to give them a haircut that gives them the *look* that suits their personality and lifestyle.

Kathleen's expenses are low. She works out of her apartment and checks her answering machine constantly. She does all of her own typing, bookkeeping and promotion work. Your office is her salon. She attributes her success to her years of business and modeling experience.

"If I'd started out as a barber, that's just what I'd be today. A barber working for someone else. My years of working in the wrong careers actually gave me all I needed to make this dream come true. It's probably a good thing that people sample other career paths first—then go back to their first love later in life. They appreciate it more. I know that I do."

Kathleen will cut your hair at your office or apartment. I asked her a very sensitive question—had any of her clients ever made a pass at her, especially since she was always in the privacy of their office? Quickly she answered, "Never." Then she thought for a minute. "Once, and I never cut his hair again. I'm very careful about picking my clients; they're all gentlemen. It's one of the best things about being my own boss."

Kathleen's ultimate dream is to open her own men's grooming salon, a very special place unlike any that now exist. She'll staff it with people like herself. She also plans on franchising her Lady Barber name. Eventually she wants to buy a house in upstate New York with a couple of Labrador retrievers running around. She'll do it, too.

What about settling down, getting married and having children? "Later," she said. "Most of my previous boyfriends have not been able to accept my drive and dedication to making my life happen. They can't accept the hours I put in; sometimes they feel as if they are not important to me." She thought deeply for a few moments. "One day I'll be where I want, or I'll meet someone who understands. I don't know. I believe in fate. It'll happen when it happens, and I'll know it's right. I'm my *first* priority now."

As busy as Kathleen's schedule is, she has a well-rounded social life, having late suppers or weekend brunches with friends. What I found amazing, despite her hectic schedule, is that she still finds time to perform community service. A volunteer for Daytop Village, Kathleen assists with yearly benefits to raise money for the foundation. She is also a volunteer for Technoserve, helping to raise money for children in Third World countries. This year she is also helping to raise money for an annual event of The New York Pops. After all this, she still finds time for her hobbies—running, reading and painting. Where does all this energy come from? "I love what I'm doing," she says. "That makes all the difference in the world. I do community work because that's what one does. Pay back."

I looked up and interviewed one of Kathleen's clients—Art Zeidman, an executive with 1010WINS radio, the number-one news radio station in New York. Art has short hair, an easy cut. Why would he not just go to a regular barber shop where he would pay $10 to $15 for his simple cut? "Kathleen makes me feel good about myself," he said, "it's something I look forward to every month."

I am now one of Kathleen's clients. At the end of our last interview, she cut my hair. I paid the full price—no freebies. From personal experience, I can tell you that her price is not expensive. I didn't get a haircut—I got an experience. Kathleen's background in modeling and acting serves her well. She entertained me as she worked on my hair. She made me laugh. For the price of a haircut, I got a cut, some therapy and a Broadway show. Afterward, I felt like I'd been undercharged. If you don't live in New York, you may want to consider flying in and renting a temporary office for the day—just so you can call the Lady Barber.

Ambassador Roy Michael Huffington: Photo by
Michael Dainard

16

A Groundswell
of Success

Roy Michael Huffington

"Keep your expenses low and always ride in the back
of the plane," Ambassador Huffington says. That's con-
servative advice from a former businessman who once
outbid all rivals for oil rights on a tract of land in Texas by
more than *double* in a sealed bidding session.

Roy Michael Huffington was born October 4, 1917, in
Tomball, Texas, a suburb of Houston. His earliest memo-
ries of childhood center around his love of the outdoors
and nature—the forests, animals, birds, rocks and trees.
When he was 12, his mother gave him a little single-action
22-caliber rifle and told him, "Now don't shoot anything
unless you're prepared to eat it." He still has the gun and
still follows his mother's advice.

At the age of 14, Roy's father was killed in an oil well
accident in South America. His mother invested the
modest insurance money and, with no prior experience,

121

did incredibly well. She was able to support Roy and his younger sister. Those were Depression days, and grown men were trying to get work of any kind. Even so, Roy managed to get a paper route to help out. Every morning at 4:00 AM, he would get up to deliver his papers. Roy kept his grades at a 98.5 average by studying before school— after delivering papers—and until 11:00 PM each night.

Roy attended grade school in Dallas and was double-promoted in the second grade. "This really messed up my grade school and high school career," he said. "I graduated from North Dallas High in mid-year and had planned to go to the University of Texas. Then I thought, I don't want to go there at mid-year, so I'll go out to SMU (Southern Methodist University), which was just a few blocks away. I had so much fun and enjoyed it so much by the end of a half-year that I stayed there for another three years."

A job as an SMU lab instructor helped Roy to cover some of the tuition expenses. He was captivated by the first course he took in geology and decided this was going to be his profession. He loved the history of the earth, the way it evolved. "The way the segments of the earth float around on an inner molten, glassy core of nickel iron was a fascinating thing to me," Roy said. "The earth was a big ball that would live and breathe. It was alive—not dead the way we might think when we look at rocks. This [the earth] was actually a moving, active planet on which we lived."

A college professor inspired Roy to go to Harvard graduate school. Although Roy had originally planned on staying only one year for a master's degree, Harvard offered him their best scholarship. "It wasn't adequate," he laughed. "It paid only $400 a year, and tuition was $440. Additionally, they gave me an alternate choice, if I wished, of being a teaching fellow; that paid $900 a year. I taught half the time and studied the other half. My tuition was only $220 a year for the half time, which left me with $680 a year to live on—rather skinny-pickings. I had to eat on $1.10 a day for the three years I was there. The ten cents was the tip for my evening meal."

Immediately after earning a Ph.D. in geology from Harvard, Roy had planned to work for the United States Geological Survey in Alaska. World War II had been going on for nearly a year. The Navy notified him that he couldn't accept the Alaska job because he would be *called up* as soon as school was out. "They didn't do that," Roy said. "I went back to SMU to write my thesis for publication. I was completely out of money and beginning to look for a job when Harvard sent a telegram asking me to come back and teach. The Navy now told me they wouldn't call me up until the next year, so I went back to Harvard as an instructor. I was there less than two months when the Navy came for me and sent me to Dartmouth for the two-month *wonder school* that was required before I could be commissioned as an officer."

In the Navy from 1942 to 1946, Roy spent the last 18 months on an aircraft carrier in the Pacific on the staff of an admiral in charge of one of the groups in Task Force 58, the fast carrier task force. Roy saw a lot of action and was awarded the Bronze Star.

Roy's carrier returned home a month or two before the war was over because of a hurricane so forceful that it wrapped the flight deck around the bow. "We had waves about 80 feet high," he recalled. "I knew that because they would come up under the flight deck that was about 80 feet above the ocean. The carrier would be picked up, then dropped down. All that could be seen was a big wall of water. At one stage I saw what I thought was a desert mirage. It seemed like a little quiver at the forward corners of the flight deck. When the next wave lifted the front of the flight deck even more, I saw the mirage again. The next time I looked, I saw the corners of the flight deck disappear. The wave just wrapped right around the bow.

I was mightily impressed with the power of the sea at that stage."

The war ended, and Roy married Phyllis Gough. If it hadn't been for the war, he probably would have ended up teaching. "I had enjoyed working with young students but realized that the $2,000 a year that they paid a beginning instructor might not be enough to support the young lady I married," he laughed. "She might be able to spend that. . . and then some. I had almost forgotten how much I liked pure geology and, therefore, decided to seek work with an oil company. I went to work for the Humble Oil & Refining Company, which is now Exxon, USA."

For the first two-and-a-half years, Roy was in New Mexico doing geological mapping in the mountains. He then spent three years in the Midland, Texas, office. Next, he was offered a promotion into the management training program under the vice president of exploration in the Houston office. There he would be exposed not only to geology and exploration but to the legal, engineering, production and refining ends of the business—all the aspects that make the oil business work.

Roy was thinking about not accepting the promotion. "I had gotten to where I thoroughly loved Midland," he said. "I knew everyone there and sort of felt I knew West Texas like the back of my hand. I went to Houston to see my boss at that time, and he said, 'Roy, make up your mind. You're a good geologist now, but we'll make an oilman out of you if you come in to the Houston office.' I made up my mind quickly because that was what I was going to do—be an oilman." Subsequently, Roy became the division exploration geologist for the Gulf Coast division.

In his new staff position, it was part of Roy's responsibility to help brief the New York-based Esso board members during their periodic checks on domestic operations. Roy's boss, by then the chairman of the board, previously had told Roy that one day he could end up on the board of directors. Roy believed that eventually this would give him the excellent opportunity to head up the Houston operation.

"Someone in Esso—I was never quite sure who—had apparently taken a liking to my talents," Roy said. "One day I got the word from Esso in New York that they wanted me to open a new exploration company headquartered in Denmark. I didn't want to get on the international circuit at that time, mostly because of the ages of our children, Michael and Terry. I was more interested in having the chance to run Houston-based Exxon than in having a shot at Esso's top job in New York City."

Roy spent a week thinking about what would happen if he turned the international promotion down. He knew he wouldn't be fired, but he felt that he would be marked for the future and that future promotions might come more slowly. Roy was in mental turmoil. He felt that his boss, the chairman, would take care of him; but he wouldn't always be there. If Roy took the promotion, he probably would be bounced around the world wherever the company wanted to send him. He would have no real control over his life. Roy asked his wife what she thought about his jumping ship and starting his own oil exploration company. "Anything you want, dear," she replied. At the age of 39, Roy tendered his resignation.

"For 18 months I didn't make a red copper cent," Roy said. "I knew I had to find a niche for myself. I was a fit geologist; I had found oil for Humble and felt I could find it for myself. But I had no real money. Ten years with the corporation had left me with only about $19,000, which wouldn't support us for long."

In those days the purchase of an oil well that would cost around $400,000 required Humble board approval. Roy began to look for one-well and two-well possibilities on the edge of already developed fields that would cost in the range of $250,000. Major oil companies wanted to develop complete fields that would cover their tremendous overhead and wouldn't be competition for these wells. The independents were digging for wells mostly in the $50,000 to $100,000 range and did not have money for more expensive wells. Roy gained credibility by quickly establishing an unbelievable record. In five years only one well out of 18 wells was dry.

The problem with being an independent is that every cent is always being rolled over into the next well. There is never a chance to build up a cash reserve. After ten years Roy ran into regulatory problems with the Federal Power Commission. They would permit only a tentative price for natural gas, which at that time was about 24 cents per thousand cubic feet. In a final administrative hearing nearly seven years later, the amount was reduced to 20.625 cents per thousand cubic feet and in another case to 18 cents. That loss and the seven-percent interest charge on the over-collected sales price were too much for Roy. He decided that, if he couldn't depend on a set price, he could no longer build his company in the United States. He decided to go overseas.

Roy looked at Indonesia, Nigeria and Iran. He met with the Iranians many times—mostly at the Plaza Hotel in New York City— but couldn't convince them that he could sell the oil if he found it. "Lucky for me," he said. "My company would have been nationalized along with everyone else, and I wouldn't be sitting here talking to you about this today."

Indonesia was another story. They didn't believe that they had any natural gas. "Well," Roy said, "they just hadn't dug deep enough." Roy and his group made one of the first trades to move into Indonesia and explore for gas and oil. In 1968 he negotiated a production sharing contract with Indonesia. Discoveries in East Kalimantan have since led to the development of a major, multibillion-dollar, liquefied natural gas (LNG) export project between Indonesia and Japan. In 1985 the Indonesian government awarded Roy the Gold Medallion Oil Pioneer Award for meritorious services to the oil and gas industry in that country.

Roy and his partners built their operation to a multi-billion-dollar size. The company eventually had a work force of over 3,500 employees and was involved in more than 60 different countries. Roy had broken his corporate bondage in order to gain some control over his own future. From the humble beginnings of financing his own education, Roy was able to make his love of geology pay off for him in more ways than just financial. Roy can read the earth and rock formations as easily as most of us can read this book.

Roy started his company on a shoestring and went 18 months without making any money. A small recession was going on at the time he started his company,and sometimes Roy thought that perhaps his timing was wrong. However, Roy believed that his nest egg was enough to keep him going for about three years if he remained frugal. The cost of living was much lower in 1956. Roy's house payments were a little more than $80 a month; he subleased office space from Arthur Young & Company.

After six months, Roy finally gained enough courage to hire a part-time secretary at $75 a month. Roy built his staff slowly over time. Everyone was a working member of the team, and people were added only as they were definitely needed. Almost everyone did more than one job; Roy attracted good people by offering them the opportunity to learn all aspects of the oil business, not just segments. Roy has always been a believer in keeping expenses low. "Always ride in the back of the plane [tourist class]," he says, "when you are starting a company."

A 14,000-foot well in the marshlands of Vermillion Parish, Louisiana, on the edge of a three-well field was the first money producer for Roy's company. Roy raised financing through the many contacts that he continued to make—networking and selling his talents and his dreams. Roy was frequently sought after by people who offered him the opportunity to head independent companies. Some had the means to help him raise money and invest in his ventures. Roy sold the gas from his first well in Vermillion Parish to the Transco Gas Pipeline Company. The well, fortunately, came in only ten feet from where Roy had originally calculated the gas sand to be. "It was blind luck," he said. "It was a real thrill to see the well come in and realize we'd be able to eat again." Finding the well was the start he needed.

Roy knew Texas, and he knows geology. As he left his office one Friday evening, Roy ran into a friend who said, "Gosh, Roy, you've got that oil production down at Dickenson. Are you going to bid on that little State tract next to yours that's coming up next Tuesday?"

Roy was surprised. He hadn't realized that the State tract was to be put up for bidding so soon. He quickly checked and verified the information. Roy then called a friend of his in Chicago—one who had helped back his well in Louisiana—to seek the investment backing he needed to bid on the land. When the friend asked how much he needed, Roy told him, "If I were still at Humble, I might bid a million for it."

On Monday morning the $1 million was wired to Roy's account. He headed to Austin where the sealed bidding was to take place on Tuesday at 10 AM. Roy kept thinking about the tract of land and how much he should bid. He realized that most people were going to think that there was only one pay there. "Since I had a well that offset it, however, I knew there were two. I decided to bid $753,000."

"The next morning I was sitting in the back of the room when the bids were opened. I was a little nervous. One of the first bids opened was for $350,000 from a company that is now known as Amoco. My former employer, Humble, bid $150,000. A lot of other small bids were opened, and then mine at $753,000. That was unheard of at the time because it came out to about $5,000 an acre. When my name was announced, I slumped down. I'd just left about $400,000 sitting on the table. I called my friend in Chicago and told him we had won the lease. He asked me how much I paid, and I told him."

"That's fine," he said. "You didn't have to spend the million. What was the next closest bid?"

With a weak voice, Roy told him.

"How could you miscalculate so badly?" his friend asked.

"You can't calculate these things sometimes, but I think it's worth it," Roy replied. "The tract paid off with four dually completed oil wells with a discovery allowable producing about 2,000 barrels of oil a day. Amoco had calculated one completion in each of the two new wells, so if you used their bid, we got the tract for a fourth of what they were willing to pay. My friend felt much better. Nobody could believe that we got so much oil out of such a tiny tract."

After that, Roy built up so much credibility that it became difficult for him to bid on leases in his own name, and he had to buy them in other people's names.

I asked Roy if he had ever considered going back into the larger corporate world. "Morgan Davis, the chairman of Humble, had told me that if things didn't work out, I could always come back. That was unheard of at Humble in those days. Usually, if you quit, you were finished forever. As nice as Morgan's gesture was, the idea was totally unacceptable to me. To go back would mean that I was admitting defeat, and I just didn't feel like a failure. Also, I was getting lots of phone calls with offers for jobs, mostly from small independent companies but also from a few larger ones. I told those who called that if I were going to work for a company, I would have stayed with my former employer. I also didn't want to be a consultant for anyone. I just wanted to go *whole-hog*, as they say, and go for broke.

"In the early months, I drove everywhere in the southern oil states and knocked on doors—introducing myself and letting people know who I was. I never took much of their time, but I knew that I had to promote myself and my new company. At the end of ten years, I had more than 20,000 names in the little black address books that took up more than three shelves in my office. I think a key to success in anything is to build up a big contact base. I have probably dealt with more than 100,000 people in the course of time I've been in business."

Roy kept in touch with Morgan Davis over the years, and when Roy made the decision to go to Indonesia, Morgan told him he was making a big mistake. Years later, when Roy had proven to be so successful, he met Morgan Davis at a business reception. Morgan Davis told him, "Roy, I really want to apologize to you: Leaving the company was the smartest thing you ever did. It's really not the same company that it used to be. It's much colder now. It has to be to compete with the rest of the industry around the world. You've done so well; everyone's proud of you. It was a good decision. I apologize for saying you were making a bad decision when you left us; it's probably the best decision you ever made in your life."

Roy mused, "Of course, that was all a look in retrospect, as to what had happened at that stage."

Roy's wife and children were his major concern, and he had their full support. His wife kept saying that whatever he wanted to do was fine, even when he told her that he might be gone for long periods of time. "If I was on the trail of something serious, I had to see it through. My wife may have regretted that from time to time as I was gone a great deal," he laughed. "On the other hand, maybe she thought it was great that I was out of the way from day to day. . ."

When the time finally came to sell and get out of the oil business, Roy decided it was time to do something else in life. "In the last decade I had been heavily involved in *not-for-profit* organizations, and I decided that I should get into a not-for-profit career. Perhaps being an ambassador was another possibility. I'd been offered an ambassadorship a time or two before but hadn't been interested because it was so much fun just building a company."

Roy had dealt with more than 60 countries, including 30 of the 34 Asian countries. He sometimes worked with countries that had three or four governments over a period of time. He was well equipped to be an ambassador.

On June 6, 1990, President Bush announced his choice to serve as United States Ambassador to Austria: Roy Michael Huffington of Houston, Texas. Roy's firm, Roy M. Huffington, Inc., had been a long-time supporter of the Salzburg Seminar educational organization, where his son Michael Huffington served on the board of directors in the early 1980s. Over the years the Huffingtons had developed a close affinity for Austria.

Untiringly, Roy continues to be actively involved in the intellectual life of the United States. In 1976 he returned to Harvard to complete its Advanced Management Program course. He is an active participant in several international affairs organizations and think tanks. Roy is an honorary life trustee of the Asia Society, having served as chairman for seven years, an honorary trustee of the Brookings Institution, a trustee of the Committee for Economic Development and a member of the Council on Foreign Relations.

Roy is currently a member of several professional societies, including the American Association of Petroleum Geologists, the Independent Petroleum Association of America and the Texas Mid-Continent Oil and Gas Association. Additionally, Roy is director of the American Petroleum Institute, a trustee of the Geological Society of

America Foundation, and he has written several publications on stratigraphic, structural and petroleum geology. Roy is a contributor of both service and financial support to U.S. civic and cultural institutions.

Currently, Roy is a trustee of Baylor College of Medicine, the Texas Medical Center, the University of Texas Health Science Center at Houston and M.D. Anderson Cancer Center. In addition to membership in the Chamber of Commerce of the United States of America and the National Petroleum Council, Roy is also an active member of the Republican Party.

In honor of his many business and civic contributions, the Houston World Trade Association named Roy Huffington International Business Leader of the Year for 1988. He also was awarded the Distinguished Service Award for 1988 from the Texas Mid-Continent Oil and Gas Association, the John Rogers Award in 1987 from the Southwestern Legal Foundation for distinguished services to both industry and civic institutions and the Golden Plate Award in 1986 from the American Academy of Achievement for Extraordinary Accomplishment in Business. In 1985 Roy received the Petroleum Industry ("Oil Drop") Award from the Petroleum Division of the American Society of Mechanical Engineers. He also has been honored with an Alumni Achievement Award from Alpha Tau Omega fraternity, Harvard Business School and an honorary Doctor of Humane Letters degree from Southern Methodist University.

Roy's daughter Terry, a geologist, has the same *rock reading* genes. A former director with Roy's company, she was very upset when it was sold. Terry started her own company and is now drilling her own oil wells in Indonesia, Turkey and Nigeria. Roy's son, Michael, is pursuing a career in politics.

Referring to my first book, *How To Market Yourself*, Roy said, "A problem is just an opportunity. Well, it really is. I think you copied something from me from 50 years earlier. I used to look at things and say, you've got a lot of problems, boy, so think of the many opportunities you've got."

Roy's advice for anyone who is unhappy doing what he or she is doing and contemplating breaking their golden handcuffs: "Life is too short to be saddled with doing something you don't like. A lot of people never decide what they want to do. They may want something easier—and *nothing* is easy. But if they know what they want to do, they should do a little advance planning. Certainly don't do what I did—jump ship in a week's time. I've told a lot of younger people that I can't think of anything worse than being miserable at what you're doing. But I also say, stay at something long enough to find out enough about it to know whether you really like it or not. You've got to have patience."

"If you don't have the support of family, like I did, you've got a real problem. It's difficult enough to start a new operation without having an unhappy family member. You see quite a few people whose marriages are ruined when their mates say that they can't put up with their work anymore because they're constantly unhappy with their job or business. That's sad; it shouldn't really happen. You can't really tell someone else what to do with their personal life; they have to decide for themselves."

When I last talked to Roy, he had just submitted his resignation to President-elect Clinton. "We all do that," he said. "It's a formality. I'm probably going to need this book now that I'll be out of a job sometime in 1993."

At 75, with all his accomplishments, you would think that the last thing Roy would be thinking about would be his next job. He certainly doesn't need to read my book; I think he was just trying to make me feel good. One of Roy's most striking character traits is that he makes people feel good. When you spend time with Roy, you feel as if you've experienced a phenomenon missing in today's hectic world. He pays attention and is interested in what you have to say. You never feel rushed in Roy's presence. He makes you feel as if you're the most important person in his life. Roy needs to take time to write a book that we could all profit from financially, mentally and spiritually.

What are Roy's future plans after leaving this post? "I don't really know. I was telling my wife the other day that maybe I'll go to Central Siberia and get back in the oil business. That's about as wild a place as I can think of. . . and she said, 'Well, lots of luck.'" He laughed. "Seriously, most of my time will be spent in the education and medical fields. I'm involved with a lot of different groups, colleges and medical centers. I reckon I've got a few things to help keep me occupied. I've also got four granddaughters with whom I'd like to spend some time. My daughter's also been asking me to do some joint ventures with her company; maybe I will. I don't think I'll ever quit working. I hope not. It's all just too much fun."

As I spent time with Ambassador Roy Michael Huffington, I became fascinated with the uncanny resemblance he bears to John Wayne—even his demeanor and speech. Considering all of his accomplishments, it is evident that Roy has the same *get it done* attitude that Wayne always portrayed in his many movie roles.

Elmore Leonard: Photo by Joan Leonard

17

Full-Time Fiction

Elmore Leonard

This past summer, Elmore Leonard finished writing his 31st book, *Pronto*, to be published in 1993. He'd like to start writing his next book in December or January and have it finished by the end of May or sometime in June. "Ideally I like to be at least 15 pages into a book by the first of the year," he said. "There are always at least a month's worth of interruptions in the spring, and it takes me about five months to write my kind of novel.

"In September of 1991, my wife and I were in London to promote *Maximum Bob*. We then went on to visit Italy. A cartoonist friend of mine told me he'd spent a week in Rapallo. That wasn't very funny, but the fact that he had been to Rapallo was reason enough for me to visit and set a part of the book there. Actually it ended up being half the book, 171 pages. I also remembered that Ezra Pound had spent a lot of time in Rapallo. So I worked Ezra Pound references into the story, and his presence becomes part of the theme."

Elmore Leonard has also written numerous short stories, more than a dozen education films and 12 screenplays. The first draft of his latest screenplay, *Stinger*, was finished in early October, 1992.

Elmore Leonard was born in New Orleans on October 11, 1925. His father worked for General Motors and was transferred several times: to Dallas, Oklahoma City, back to Dallas, then to Detroit, where Elmore started the first grade. The next transfer took the family to Memphis where Elmore attended the second, third and part of the fourth grades. In 1934 the family moved back to Detroit where Elmore has lived ever since.

When he was six, Elmore remembers wanting to be a cowboy or a pirate (a *good* pirate). By age ten he wanted to be a soldier. "I remember while I was in grade school," he said, "the Spanish Civil War was going on, and I would fantasize that the school was under siege, surrounded by the enemy. It was up to someone to get out through their lines and bring up the relief column. I was always the one who volunteered."

By the time he was 15, Elmore wanted to be a major league baseball player. "I knew I wouldn't make it, though, because I was a weak hitter—I had trouble seeing the ball. Once I started wearing glasses, I didn't think it was possible to play professionally. At that time probably no more than one or two guys in the majors wore glasses. I played first base, mainly because I throw left-handed, although I write right-handed."

In high school, the Jesuit-run University of Detroit High, Elmore played football—center his junior year and quarterback as a senior—as well as baseball. "At that time the school competed in Detroit's Class A City League. I didn't have the size, but I really liked it; I had the desire and the drive, and you could get by on that back then."

Elmore considers this Jesuit high school experience as the most important aspect of his education: "[the school] was where learning, reading and investigating became part of my life and where I learned how to think—to ask questions—not just *what* but *why*."

Elmore tried to join the Marines when he was 17, but he failed the eye exam. Later he was drafted into the Navy where he went to service school in Norfolk and came out a Seaman First Class. He was shipped overseas to New Guinea, then to a Construction Battalion (CB) outfit on Los Negros in the Admiralty Islands where an airstrip was maintained. The unit moved to the Philippines following the bombing of Hiroshima and Nagasaki. "When the war ended, we were each given two cases of beer," he laughed. "We went outside and drank them."

After the war, Elmore enrolled at the University of Detroit and took courses that he liked. "I majored in English," he said. "I didn't know what I wanted to do though I thought I wanted to write. That seemed always to be in the back of my mind." He had written his first play when he was in the fifth grade. It came out of having read parts of *All Quiet on the Western Front*, which had been serialized in the *Detroit Times*. It was a World War I play and, utilizing his classmates, Elmore put it on for a small audience that consisted of his teacher and the Mother Superior. "I'm surprised they let me do it," he said. "I don't know where it [the script] is; I'd love to have it." That was the only writing Elmore had done until college.

Elmore's freshman English instructor told the class that anyone who submitted a short story to the Writers Club contest, *The Manuscribblers*, would automatically receive a *B* in English. Elmore's submission finished in the top ten. "The prize," he said, "was a critique by an author's agent located in Detroit. It wasn't too long before I realized there was no such thing as an author's agent in Detroit at that time. She pointed out that I had written the thing in the second person, using *you* all the way, and

I don't think that was ever successful up until Jay McInerney wrote *Bright Lights, Big City*."

Two years later, Elmore entered the contest again and won second place. "I didn't win anything that I can remember, but the judge—of all people—was John Farrow, Mia Farrow's father, a film director. One of his best works was *Hondo*, starring John Wayne."

Elmore's father had been with General Motors for most of his working life. In 1948 he left the security of a large corporation to open a Chevrolet, Buick and Oldsmobile dealership in Las Cruces, New Mexico. It couldn't have been a better time since people needed cars after the war. Elmore was to come to work for him and eventually take over the business.

"It really appealed to me at the time," Elmore said, "I don't know why. I guess it was the idea of making money, getting married, everything just falling into place—doing what everybody else was doing."

Unfortunately, Elmore's father died just six months after opening the dealership. With the help of his brother-in-law, Elmore tried to hang on to his father's equity. The Chevrolet regional manager, an old friend of Elmore's father's, asked him what else interested him.

"I mentioned writing though at that time I'd written only the two stories while at the University of Detroit and sold nothing. The regional manager asked if I'd ever thought about advertising. I said, 'Gee, I don't know. Maybe.'"

The regional manager gave him the name of a vice president at Campbell-Ewald, Chevrolet's ad agency, and Elmore met with him when he returned to Detroit. The VP asked if he had ever thought about media. "I'd never even heard the word," Elmore said. "It wasn't used the way it is now. I didn't even know it was the plural of *medium*. I said, 'Oh, sure, and kept bugging him until he finally gave me a job in office services, which was delivering mail and memos, running errands. That was my entry into the corporate world of advertising. It was September of 1949, and I had just gotten married that previous July."

It wasn't until the next year that Elmore started seriously thinking about writing. "I felt I should pick a genre," he said, "crime, detective or western fiction, an area in which to learn how to write. I decided on westerns because of the wide-open market for western movies at that time, as well as magazine stories."

Elmore wrote several short stories and submitted them to pulp magazines. He got rejected and decided he had to go about it in a much more professional way. He decided to pick out an area and time and to research both thoroughly. He chose the Southwest, researched Arizona in the 1880s, the cavalry, Apache Indians, read such books as *The Truth about Geronimo* and *On the Border with Crook*. He studied reference books on cowboys, what they wore, even what kind of coffee they drank. He also subscribed to *Arizona Highways* magazine and relied on its scenic photography for his descriptions of the country. The research served him well.

Elmore's next story was submitted to *Argosy* magazine. Even though they rejected the story, *Argosy* said they liked the way he wrote, and to please submit anything else he had written that took place in that period.

"I sat down and wrote a novelette, *Apache Agent*, and they bought it. Their letter said, 'Dear Mr. Leonard, I am happy to report that your novelette, *Apache Agent*, is one that we like very much. We should like to pay you $1,000 for the first and second North American serial rights. I hope this is agreeable to you. Can you send me some information about yourself, some biographical material and some informal snapshots which we plan to use in our *Argonotes*? By all means let us see some more fiction. Sincerely, John Bender, Associate Editor.' "

The short story that was originally rejected was passed on to one of *Argosy's* western magazines. They bought it for only $100, but the editor wrote Elmore a four-page letter that was both encouraging and practical. He suggested that even with his early success, Elmore should not think about quitting his job with the ad agency. The editor felt that if Elmore quit too early, he would turn into a hack and start grinding work out. He felt that Elmore showed too much promise and didn't want him to fall into the trap of churning out stories just to make a living.

"But I was already chomping at the bit. I wasn't even writing ad copy at the time," Elmore said. "I left Campbell-Ewald as an office boy to join a smaller agency as a writer. After 15 months I returned to Campbell-Ewald as a writer. It's funny. When I had left, everyone was on a *Mr.* basis. When I returned as a writer, we were on a first-name basis. I wrote Chevrolet ads for the next seven years until my profit sharing came due, and I took the money and left. This was March of 1961, and I had been preparing for it."

Elmore had only one small account when he left as well as a film producer friend who had a contract with Encyclopedia Britannica Films. Elmore wrote a dozen screenplays for the film producer and also wrote a recruitment film, *The Man Who Has Everything,* for the Franciscan order to recruit brothers.

"I left the agency to write full-time," he said. "I had written about 30 short stories and five books and had made even a couple of movie sales by then. My first wife and I decided to move into a bigger house, and there went the profit sharing. All of a sudden I needed money, so I had to hustle up some free-lance advertising work. The movies for Britannica helped—about $1,000 each—but I figured I needed about $2,000 a month. I didn't get back into fiction until 1966 when *Hombre* sold to Fox, and that sold for only $10,000. That gave me about six months."

Elmore still handled a couple of advertising accounts, Eton Chemical Company and Hurst Performance Products. "*Hombre* had just sold, and I decided I had to write a book. It was *Mother, This is Jack Ryan.* Nobody liked the title. My New York agent was sick at the time, and she sent the book out to H. N. Swanson in Hollywood who had negotiated the two movie sales. Swanie called me after reading the manuscript, my first nonwestern, and said, 'Kiddo, I'm going to make you rich.' He then got 84 rejections in the next few months. They were all rejecting it, they said, because it was a downer. My main character was an anti-hero who couldn't get into the Army and ended up becoming a burglar. But I loved this kind of character. I spent five or six months rewriting the manuscript and fell behind on paying my media bills for my ad accounts, using the money to live on as I spent the time writing. I think about this as the time I made my run. It was risky—what I wrote had to sell and not just for a few bucks. Fortunately, it did. Film rights sold for $50,000, and I was back in the fiction business, finally out of advertising completely.

"What I was writing in the 1950s was selling, but it was mostly to the pulps. I did sell one story to *The Saturday Evening Post* and several to *Argosy*. I was doing okay, selling everything I wrote. Then I experienced that barren period between 1961 and 1966 when I didn't write any fiction at all and was afraid I might never get back into it. But I definitely did not want to go back to work in the corporate world. If I did, it would have to be on my terms, at my own agency. I had a friend at J. Walter Thompson on the Ford account, and we would talk about forming our own agency, but he would never do it. He liked the big agency life, the corporate level, working with creative people. It's funny that word is used so much in the advertising business, more than anywhere, and it may be the least creative world you can work in. I mean, as far as creativity is concerned. I didn't like the fact that you had to write a certain way. During the time I was doing Chevy ads, they had to be sprightly, full of alliteration, with all kinds of similes and metaphors, and that isn't the way I write."

In 1962, needing money, Elmore went back to Campbell-Ewald to see about working there again. The creative director told him he had to commit to at least five years. "Looking at the kind of writing they wanted," he said, "the five years sounded like a sentence. The creative director recommended that I take some time off and think about it. So I went skiing for a week, came back with new energy and wrote a brochure, 'Free-lance Writer with Fresh Ideas.' I mailed out 200 hundred copies to small agencies and art studios and got about 20 jobs to keep me going."

Elmore's writing habits started when he was still working for the ad agency. He would get up at 5:00 AM and write two pages before going to work.

"It took me several months," he said, " to get up the first time after setting the alarm. It was always so dark and cold that I just didn't want to get up and write. Finally, I made myself do it. I had a rule—I had to start writing before I put the water on for coffee; otherwise I could waste valuable minutes standing in the kitchen reading a magazine while I waited for the coffee. So I had to write something first, at least a paragraph, and I did. I wrote two pages every day. A page an hour. This is much better than I do now. If I wrote a page an hour now, I could write a book in two months. Now it takes me from 9:30 in the morning until 6:00 PM to write seldom more than four pages. I guess because I keep trying to make it better. At least having developed a style, which took about ten years, I know exactly the sound I want my writing to have."

In 1985 Elmore Leonard made *The New York Times* bestseller list with his novel, *Glitz*.

"It was never a goal," he said. "It did, of course, sell more books, which means more people are reading what I write, and I'm happy about that. I've always considered what I do more commercial than literary, motivated more by the idea of making money than writing literature. I'm always surprised to find out that certain literary writers do read my work. It's extremely flattering."

Elmore has this advice for people considering making a move toward what they would really like to do: "If I hadn't made a change, I'd probably be dead. Or I'd be running my own ad agency. I remember one winter night in the 1950s coming home from work. I walked in the door, and my publisher was on the phone. I still had my coat on and remember being wet and miserable while he listed the things wrong with a manuscript I'd recently submitted. Right after dinner, I went down to the basement where I had an office and began revising the manuscript, a western. I remember vividly that I didn't feel at all like working on it, but I did because I was determined that some day I'd become a full-time fiction writer. Everyone seemed to be trying to discourage me—my agent, my editors—but I had to do it. The desire was too strong not to.

"Every once in a while, an interviewer—a newspaper or magazine writer—will tell me how lucky I am, that I have the best job in the world. I can write exactly what I want and be paid a lot of money for it. (A friend who writes in the same genre, Robert Parker, says, "As we both know, luck has little to do with it.") I do agree with the interviewer that even after working hard at my craft for so many years I *am* lucky, or my timing was just right in the mid-1980s when, after 30 years, I was finally *discovered* and became an overnight success. I'm so glad that back in the 1960s, when I began writing fiction again, I took a chance and made my run. If I hadn't, I'd still be doing it part-time, if at all. You need support, encouragement, but more than anything else, you need the determination to do it, to leave security behind and take a chance. You'll never know, will you, unless you try."

Mark Christopher Lingley: Photo by Michael Dainard

18

Golden Needles

Mark Christopher Lingley

"Good clothes open all doors."

Thomas Fuller

"Clothes don't make the man, but clothes have got many a man a good job."

Herbert Harold Vreeland

Without realizing it, Mark Christopher Lingley has found that both of these quotes have had a double meaning in his life. Mark loves good clothes and dresses well, but designing and making good clothes opened all doors and gave him a wonderful new career.

The doors Mark chose were probably the hardest ones in the world to crack open. He owns Mark Christopher of Wall Street, a custom shirt maker with a solid customer base that includes mainly top executives in the financial district. His showroom is located at 87 Nassau Street, but many of his customers are much too busy to visit for fittings. Mark goes to their offices—even the trading floor of the New York Stock Exchange—armed with a tape measure and a selection of fabrics. He takes more than 20 measurements—of each client's neck, arms, wrists, chest, waist, hips, back, shoulders and more. What he delivers back to his customer is a quality custom shirt that is a perfect fit in every way.

Mark was born in Wakefield, Massachusetts, in 1955. His father was a truck driver for the Navy, and his mother, a nurse. He has two sisters and a brother. Mark attended grade school in Wakefield, and he dreamed of becoming an airline pilot. The family moved to Boston, and Mark attended junior high and high school there. The family lived right across from Harvard Square, and Mark's first full-time job, which enabled him to finance his education at Harvard, was as admissions secretary for Harvard Law School. At that time, Mark's dream was to become a writer, and his first two years he majored in English.

"It's still something I want to pursue later in life," Mark says. "I want to write romances—Gothic, something along the lines of Barbara Cartland."

Mark's job at Harvard was his first taste of corporate life and working for others. He came to despise it because it was so political.

Mostly on a whim, Mark decided to take a tailoring course at the Cambridge Center for Adult Education on Harvard Square. He had lost the first real love of his life, and he was searching for someone or something to fill the void. Not able to find another person, he turned to something that would occupy his hands as well as his mind. One day he sat down and sewed a shirt completely by hand. It totally changed his life. He still doesn't know how or why, but it became the new love of his life, almost an obsession. His first effort at making a jacket, however, was a joke.

"It was a pinstripe," he laughed, "and I sewed everything right except the left sleeve. It was inside out. So there I had a whole new look. Everyone loved it. It was hysterical."

Mark decided to pursue his new love. He left Harvard and enrolled in a two-year fashion design program at Chamberlain Design School. The courses all concentrated on women's fashion, and Mark had to really control his own curriculum. He was the only male in the class, and all he really wanted to do was design and make shirts.

"They all thought I was crazy to do it," he said. "Most of the classes were filled with homemakers, but I really did learn the basics of design and disciplines of crafting there. It was a good school."

When he graduated from Chamberlain and left his job in the admissions office at Harvard, Mark swore that he would never get another corporate job. He felt that his design talents were a little too far ahead for Boston. He had managed to save quite a bit of money, so he headed for San Francisco. On the way, he stopped in New York and fell in love with the city. He never left.

Mark's first week in New York was fascinating. He is very outgoing and friendly, and he met many new friends. That led to an offer of a job as a waiter in a very exclusive restaurant on the Upper East side that catered to the rich and famous, such as the Kissingers, Richard Nixon and Jackie Onassis. Mark worked there as headwaiter for seven years, making a lot of money.

Two years later, Mark enrolled at the Fashion Institute of Technology, taking night courses in menswear designing and graduated with a bachelor of arts. After that he became very bored. He was making excellent money as a headwaiter, but he was working for someone else, and in its own way the setting was very corporate.

Mark said, "I also knew that I wanted to design and make shirts. I was growing older and had to make some kind of move."

New York is an expensive place to live, and even though Mark was making a good salary, it took most of his money to live in the city. When he had first come to New York, he had $10,000 in savings, but most of that went toward setting up an apartment and paying for school. At this point, he had exactly $1,000 left in his savings account.

Mark found a small space in a five-floor walk-up one block from where he is currently located. He took his last $1,000 and paid the rent and security. It was an empty room with no electricity, no furniture and no machinery. His sister was a flight attendant, and she brought a lot of her very pretty colleagues to hand out flyers on the street.

Mark's first customer was a man who walked up the five flights of stairs. "Thank God it was a bright day," Mark laughed. "Otherwise the poor man would have been in a pitch black, empty studio. I had nothing, no samples, no fabrics, nothing, just me in an empty room with a tape measure, but I sold him a shirt; it was a green gingham."

Mark made the shirt in his apartment, but a week later when the man was to come back for the shirt, something had spilled on it. So Mark had it soaking in a pail of water. When the man knocked at the door, Mark was terrified to open it. Somehow he got through it all, and the man was pleased. Mark had his first sale, but it raised a real question in his mind. "Do I want people to come up here?" Mark asked. "No, I don't think it's the appropriate image for what I want to project."

Mark had a close friend in Boston who had recently opened her own real estate business. She advised Mark to have some really nice direct mail pieces made up and send them out. She even helped Mark write and design the piece. Mark positioned himself as a custom shirtmaker who made office calls. Two weeks after his mailing, he received a call from a man in an office a block away. Armed with a sample book of fabrics, Mark sold the man more than $1,000 worth of shirts. Direct mail became the crucial marketing ploy of Mark's new company.

Mark still worked as a headwaiter at night and tried to build his business during the day. He poured all the money he made into the new business—rent, machines, people and mailing costs. He had to work to support his new business. It was a constant anxiety run every afternoon to make the 4:05 PM train that would get him to the restaurant at 4:30 PM. He didn't dare be late too many times, or his boss would fire him.

Mark struggled, and business grew slowly for the first few years. He made the patterns, did the cutting and managed to find good seamstresses to sew for him. At the same time, Mark continued to try to build a customer base and service it. He built his mailing list by going into the lobbies of buildings in the financial district and copying names from the directories. It was the early 1980s, when money was plentiful and optimism heady around Wall Street. Mark was determined to tap into his share of it.

Mark lived in constant chaos for five years as he slowly worked on his dream. One day it became evident to the owner of the restaurant that Mark's real attention was on his new business. Mark admits that he used the job to solicit new customers for his shirts. "After all," he said, "the clientele at the restaurant was my target market. I even told [Richard] Nixon what I was doing. It was hard for me not to talk about it. It was the thing that I loved. I was well-liked by a lot of my customers, and it was from some of them that I got the seed money to really start to grow the company."

Mark hated his work at the restaurant. He loved his customers, and good friendly service came naturally to him, but the atmosphere of the restaurant itself was suffocating. Mark's boss was extremely tough, and his fellow employees were always undermining each other to get better treatment or raises.

"I was a perfect target," he said, "because as head-waiter I made the most money."

Mark knew that he would eventually have to leave the restaurant and work in his business full-time if he wanted to really make it grow.

"But it was scary," he said, "because as much as I hated my job, it was still my bread and butter."

The decision was made for him. The owner didn't fire him, but he rearranged the schedule so that Mark would have to work more days.

"I had to make a decision at that point. He knew what he was doing," Mark said, "and he was determined to make it rough for me. I had some investors, and I just walked. Looking back, it was a blessing in disguise, because now my business had to grow and support me. If it had happened sooner, I probably would have grown quicker. I should really go back and thank my ex-boss."

What Mark was most afraid of was the timing. It was early in 1988, and Wall Street had crashed in October 1987. Some of Mark's previous clientele who had been making $400,000 a year were now trying to get jobs as cab drivers.

"These guys weren't in the market for $165 shirts anymore," he laughed. "They were trying to sell their old ones."

Despite the hard times on Wall Street, Mark's business continued to grow. Now that he was putting all his time and energy into the business, it was paying off. He did a lot of networking and started courting the media. Articles began appearing in major publications, and his business prospered.

"It was really word of mouth that grew my business," Mark said in reflection. "People liked my work and told their friends. Even people who had lost their jobs had passed me on to the CEOs of their companies."

Mark's clientele included people such as Randolph and Patty Hearst; Robert De Niro; Douglas Brandrup, president of The Metropolitan Club; Joseph J. Grano, Jr., president of retail sales for PaineWebber; Stephen Rothchild Simone, vice president at PaineWebber; and Josiah Low, managing director of investment banking at Donaldson, Lufkin & Jenerette.

Mark expanded his custom shirt business to include ties made from remnants purchased from small fabric houses off Seventh Avenue. It's rare to find someone else wearing a tie just like the one you buy from Mark. They aren't mass produced. He now sells custom-made suspenders, sports shirts, underwear, robes and suits. Shirts range from $85 to $225, suits average $1,300 and ties $65 to $85. Mark is contemplating lowering the cost of his ties to increase volume.

"It's an impulse item," Mark said, "and at a lower cost I'll probably sell more to the same customer. It's amazing the difference a new tie will make in the look of your wardrobe. It's an inexpensive way to perk up your look."

Mark's shirts and accessories are now being sold in stores like Saks Fifth Avenue and Barney's. Henri Bendel carries Mark's custom-designed women's robes at around $650. On October 1, 1992, Mark opened his first store at 26 Broadway. This interview took place the afternoon of September 30. I was amazed at the pure, raw energy Mark exhibited as he juggled the interview while giving his staff instructions, giving personal attention to two customers who came in for fittings, making phone calls and trips (with me following) to his new store to make sure all was ready for the next morning's opening. Through it all, Mark seemed to have an inner calmness that he was unwilling to admit, even to himself.

Mark feels that his biggest weakness is being a perfectionist. It's very hard for him to turn work over to others.

"I'm working at it," he said. "I'm getting better at trusting other people with tasks that I used to handle when we were a small company."

Even though Mark's parents were not from the corporate world, his grandparents were. His grandfather headed up the Boston Main Railroad, and his grandmother was a businesswoman in her own right. Mark feels that their genes probably skipped a generation to him. Mark considers himself a risk taker, and that must have come from his grandfather. Mark's aunt told him the story of how his grandfather became such a successful businessman.

"He was always a little crazy," Mark said. "He was always taking risks. He was a Canadian—in fact there's a small town named after him, Lingleyville, somewhere near Prince Edward Island. Anyway, they had built a bridge, and they needed someone to drive a locomotive across it to see if it would hold the weight. Nobody wanted to do it. My grandfather volunteered. He could have been killed, but he did it. From that day on, he kept getting promoted."

Mark's grandmother owned and operated a general store in Wakefield, and Mark feels that he obtained a lot of his business knowledge from her.

"She taught me a lot," he said. "As a child I remember she always had us [the children in the family] play store, and for some reason I was always the leader. She taught me about business. My mother was a major influence also. She always pushed me in the right direction—the right schools to go to. She was very concerned that I receive the right education."

Mark plans to continue expanding his business but in a slow and careful manner. "I don't want to move so quickly that I risk lowering my quality standards because I'm too busy overseeing expansion. I can't give any less attention to our regular customers. That's going to be the hardest part for me. I'm a real people pleaser. I want people to be happy with my work and service."

The other thing that bothers Mark is where he will find quality manufacturing for his ready-to-wear lines. He wants to keep everything in the United States, but it seems harder and harder to make that happen. Even top designers such as Calvin Klein were forced to go outside the country.

"Even fabrics," he said, "like cotton—at one time, the best cotton in the world came from America, but today it's coming from Europe and Japan. I have to buy the fabrics that meet my quality standards. That's what makes me unique. There's no way I can compromise on quality to make a few extra bucks. That's not what Mark Christopher is all about. Mark Christopher is me, and I care what people think about me."

It's obvious that Mark loves what he's doing. He feels that there aren't enough hours in the day to accomplish everything he wants to do. He had only a few words of advice for someone who is *successfully unhappy* in corporate bondage.

"Just go for it." Mark said. "If you've got a dream, make a plan to make it happen."

Scott Powers: Photo by Michael Dainard

In Production

Scott Powers

When you walk into Scott Powers's office, the first thing that comes to mind is that this man does nothing. No papers are lying on his desk, and everything is in its place. The lights are soft and low, and even the computer is turned off. Scott is as immaculate as his office. What does this man do? He does a little bit of a lot of things, and that's just the way he wants it. Scott Powers Productions, Inc. has three full-time employees, but it is a mini-conglomerate of sorts. Scott utilizes up to 30 people on a free-lance basis as they are needed.

Scott is a model and an actor. He trains models. He is an agent. His company is also an advertising agency and a production company. Scott is a partner in a voice coaching school—and on and on. If it interests Scott, he gets involved.

Scott was born in Chicago, but he grew up on the north shore of Long Island, better known as *The Gold Coast*. In high school his interests were tennis, social life, creativity and acting. In college he majored in television and radio communications.

Scott's dream was to be an actor, but he grew up in a family and social stratum that expected the men to go off to the corporate world (his father was a prominent executive) each day and the women to play tennis or lunch at the club. That's what one did! In this very upscale, rarefied lifestyle, people owned or ran companies—the arts were only what one did for a hobby.

Scott remembered his first day in high school. "People asked me what my father's title was, what kind of cars we owned and what club(s) my family belonged to. If I could pass those three tests, I could be allowed to talk about other *human* or social subjects."

Even the high school dances were special. It wasn't unusual for one of the parents—a senior executive with a major airline—to have an airplane fuselage brought in for atmosphere. Scott's community was known for the highest alcohol consumption per capita in the United States. People who lived there were used to seeing themselves in the papers and having books written about their community. The children were all told that they were very special people— there was no one else like them.

Scott's dream to be an actor had to be stifled. He said, "Do you do what you want to do, or do you want to pay your rent? I lived in a society where it was expected that you wouldn't necessarily do what you wanted to do because one had obligations. You *had* to fulfill your obligations first. It wasn't until later in life that I found out you could do what you wanted and still fulfill your obligations."

While Scott was in college, he took a summer job as a production assistant with a film company. "It was the 1960s; there was lots of money around. It was glamorous. It was everything I ever expected." Scott graduated with an MBA; his thesis was on network television programming.

Scott's first full-time job was with an advertising agency as an assistant producer for TV and radio shows and commercials. He kept moving from agency to agency, production company to production company—up, up and up in the corporate world to become a producer and account supervisor.

"You had to move around a lot," he said. "If you're with an agency too long, you're not considered very good—stale."

Disenchantment started setting in the higher up Scott moved in title and salary. He wasn't doing as much of the creative as he wanted. It became just a job, not a career—a corporate grind with days of repetition. "I thought I was basically stagnating mentally and career-wise," he reflected. "It was suffocating, and my work environment became more involved with the preservation of my job."

Scott felt he was working with people above him who weren't terribly talented. They were there for reasons other than their talent. He began to realize that he was not in control of his own destiny. "Were we in advertising or what?" he said.

Scott was asked to do a lot of unpleasant things to keep clients. When he objected, he was told by one very important client that he could be replaced on the account in less than 15 minutes. Scott went to his boss at the agency, hoping for support. His boss looked him straight in the eye and said, "Scott, you are in charge of the most profitable account with this agency, and we have every intention of keeping it—with or without you. We're nothing but well-paid whores in Brooks Brothers suits."

This was the turning point in Scott's corporate life. He said, "This is not how I want to earn a living." He was 36 and felt that he had spent the better part of his life doing everything the way someone else wanted him to do it—his life, his school and his career.

"I could no longer justify [to myself] working with people like that," he said. "I looked around at other people in the agency and saw that none of them had a healthy relationship. None of them led a healthy life. They were all screwed up in one way or another. I can screw up on my own and be happier. I don't have to be in this garbage."

Scott realized that he was entrepreneurial by nature and could make his own opportunities rather than have his whole life laid out for him like it had been since birth. He wasn't the kind of person who responded well to people telling him what he should do. "I bridle against someone telling me I can go to lunch only from 12:30 PM to 1:30 PM," he said. "I'm an adult. I don't like that kind of rigidity. If I'm working on an important project, I feel I can decide to go earlier, later or not at all."

Scott was making an extremely large salary when he decided to make his escape from the corporate world. He also enjoyed a high profile lifestyle with a generous expense account. From the outside, it appeared that Scott not only had the world on a string but could make it do tricks. But Scott was not happy. His biggest fear was that if he stayed in the business, he might become just like the people he despised. He had to get out.

Scott didn't make any preparations; he just left. "I'll find a way to do it," he said.

He knew himself very well. If he had had a large financial cushion to fall back on, he feels he would have floundered around. Scott was used to a very good lifestyle, and he had no intention of giving it up. He felt that he needed the anxiety to help push him forward. It forced him to be very resourceful quickly. When the American Express bill, car payment and other bills came due, he knew his only alternative would be bankruptcy. What sustained him in the beginning was performing. He did commercials, modeling and some roles on television. While doing this to support himself, he formed his new company.

Scott had learned that as an actor, people tended to think of him as having no *real* profession. It's very hard to rent a car, get credit cards, obtain a mortgage or do all those other things that having a *corporate* job allows you to do. With that in mind, Scott opened Scott Powers Productions, Inc. as the mantle to wrap around himself. He became a *corporation*.

Scott's company does many different things, but they are the things that interest Scott. In addition to being a company that promotes Scott himself as a performer, the company produces radio and TV commercials, cast consults to agencies and clients, conducts classes in commercial print modeling, produces seminars for the entertainment industry and rents studio space for training and special classes. Scott's philosophy is to look for a niche in the market and then to fill it.

Scott always seems to be looking for opportunities. Recently he went on vacation to a small island in the West Indies. One of the first things he noticed was that the brochure for the resort seemed a little dated and didn't do justice to the resort. He approached the owners and ended up with a new account. Within weeks of returning to work, Scott had redesigned their brochure and was flying models and a crew of 18 down for a *working* vacation. While in post-production for the brochure, Scott pitched the resort's public relations account. He won that, too.

Scott is not exactly where he would like ultimately to be, but it's a matter of building little by little. "As long as I see progress," he said, " I'm happy. The most pleasurable aspect is knowing that the progress is something that is the result of my own efforts. I am in total control of my own destiny. I'm no longer a puppet of the corporate world."

Scott had very little support when he made the decision to go out on his own. His family was totally against it. His co-workers were adamant in their opinion that he would return to the corporate fold within months of not having a generous expense account and all the other perks.

Scott admitted that it was very rough in the beginning, but over time he has been able to recover the perks and so much more. Some months he had to depend upon *creative financing* to get him through. His attitude was simply that he *had* to make it, and the worst possible thing that could happen to him was that he would have to end up getting another job, even if it was flipping hamburgers, to pay the rent.

Scott now works much harder today then he did in his corporate job. Many days he's still working at midnight. The difference he feels is that he is doing productive work—work that he wants to do—and it's his decision.

Scott is also writing a book, *Commercial Print: The Actor's Guide to Survival* (working title), published by Heinemann in 1993. Scott was one of only six people who took the most dangerous Grand Canyon white water trip available this year. He's not afraid to take risks.

Scott's office and desk are so clean because he is extremely organized and uses a computer. "It's the only way I can keep track of all the projects I'm involved in," he said. "If I'm not working on it, it's filed away."

Scott's advice for others is: Don't wait too long to make a move. If someone is really unhappy with their current job or career, they should plan their escape and just do it—especially if the person is around 40. People have to realize that they are in their most productive years and that it's all going to end someday. It's much better to spend those years doing the things you really want to do. "It's not for everybody, though," he counsels. "Some people flourish in an environment where everything is provided for them and they are told what to do. This type of person will probably not make it, because when you first go out on your own, you have to do everything yourself. You have to be self-driven and self-motivated."

Scott knows that in today's world you cannot afford to be a one-idea person. He believes in making things happen. His greatest tool is the telephone, and he communicates constantly with other people. He is very observant and receptive to people and things around him; that's how he finds the opportunities. He feels his greatest strength is that he never procrastinates—ever. "If it needs to be done," he said, "then go do it."

Scott's father retired when he was 55 and hasn't done anything since then. He's now 70 and has spent the last 15 years sitting in a chair waiting for the end. That's not how Scott wants to end his career or his life.

"I couldn't be more opposite. I love what I'm doing today. I'll work until the very end," Scott said, "until I'm cold. If I died today at 44, I'd feel very fulfilled. But if I die at age 75 or so, I want the next 31 years to be filled with new and exciting experiences. Morbid as it may sound, I'll probably find a way to be doing something, even as my body starts to cool."

David Grant Roth: Photo by Michael Dainard

At the Easel

David Grant Roth

If you want a David Grant Roth painting, be prepared to spend $4,000 to $8,000. David sells enough of them to make a very comfortable living. He started painting full-time at the age of 49! One day David yelled, "CUT!" and quit an extremely successful career as a director for television. When he broke his corporate bondage, he was a full-time director for two popular shows—*Sesame Street* and the soap opera, *Secret Storm*. Money, power, prestige and glamour didn't hack it. David *needed* to paint.

David was born in 1923, in a small town in upstate New York, and spent most of his early childhood near Buffalo. He went to high school in Franklinville where his father was an agricultural teacher.

In grade school when he found that he could make drawings of his classmates and teachers that were pretty good likenesses, David discovered his talent for art. He studied art all the way through school.

David attended college at Syracuse University for two years, then went into the Marine Corps for four years. When he returned to Syracuse University, it was very crowded. It had grown from about 6,000 to 12,000 students, and some were taking classes in Quonset huts set up on campus. David's G.I. bill didn't come through for quite some time, and he was broke. He got a part-time job as a stock boy at Woolworth's and cleaned classrooms at The Fine Arts College—he'd do anything to earn money to live on. One winter day, as he was shoveling snow in front of the store, a friend of his from the Marines—a captain— came along and said, "Dave Roth, what are you doing shoveling snow in front of Woolworth's? Geez, you ought to be able to do something better than this. This is awful." David started thinking afterward that the captain was right—he should be able to find something better to do.

David had always been a pretty good portrait artist. He contacted another friend from the Marine Corps and made a proposition. His friend was one of the few people David knew who had a phone in those days. David asked his friend to be his agent. David was going to become a portrait artist. His flair for arrogance came early—he told his friend that he would commission the portraits, but that the *artist* doesn't talk to anybody until he gets on site.

"You tell them," David said, "that the artist is very temperamental, very difficult. That's the way he is. But he's a great artist." David built an entire image, including not wearing socks when it was snowing. He didn't really have a portfolio at the time, nothing in oils. Most of David's work had been in pastels and charcoal. He made up some story that he didn't use oils because they were too cumbersome.

When David was doing a portrait, he wouldn't let his subject see it until it was completed. This was another part of his arrogance. He made this a rule because if the sketch wasn't going well at the first sitting, he didn't want the subject to discover this. One woman insisted that she see her portrait in progress. David told her no. She got up and started over to the easel. David slammed the painting into his case, stood up and said, "No! That's it. I won't come back. I told you from the beginning." David walked out. The woman called and begged him to come back; she would abide by his rules. He came back and finished the portrait. David said there was no way he could have let her see the total disaster of his first try, "She would have thrown me out. My facade and reputation would have been ruined."

David got a big write-up in the local Sunday paper. He made a living at painting for the rest of the time he was studying at Syracuse. But David was not destined to become a working artist yet. He was studying philosophy and was a pre-ministerial student. He constantly fluctuated between wanting to become an artist and wanting to become a minister.

He didn't really like Syracuse anymore because it was so crowded. He met with the minister from his hometown and asked his advice. The minister recommended Tusculum College in Tennessee. It had the reputation for having a great philosophy department, and any student from there could get into Princeton or any other seminary. David transferred from Syracuse to Tusculum and went to Tennessee to study to become a minister.

David was going to start a brand-new life. He was going to study hard and do a lot of drawing and painting. He was going to become a hermit, just paint and study. Fate stepped in, and he received a call from the head of the drama department at Tusculum, who was also the daughter of his philosophy professor. She wanted David to be in her play that fall, *The Glass Menagerie*, and play the part of Tom. At first he didn't want to have anything to do with it, but she was beautiful and very persuasive. David finally agreed, and before he knew it, he was in love with acting, the theater *and* the head of the drama department. David was good at acting and started getting involved more and more with the theater. He learned everything from acting—set design, lighting, production and finally, directing.

During this time as a student minister, David was also preaching at three different rural churches using the college Jeep to make his rounds. He also did quite a bit of painting, including several murals. David had three different and distinct career paths that he could have pursued—artist, minister or actor.

The head of the drama department moved to New York; David followed. He now considered himself an actor and scrambled around New York trying to get established. This was 1949–1950; television was in its infancy. A friend of David's, a cameraman working on *Studio One*, contacted him because the director of *Studio One* wanted to have a portrait of his daughter done. David did the portrait, then told the director he didn't want money. He wanted an acting part in *Studio One*. David had bartered his way into acting and even had the opportunity to act with Ann Bancroft.

David landed a job with the School for Radio and Television as an actor. Within a short period of time, he was in charge of hiring other actors to perform in the short pieces that allowed the students to learn production. In this capacity he met his future wife, a model and actress named Bonnie Barton. Here David learned the craft of directing while acting. He watched and learned every aspect of television production. One day the instructor for directing was ill and asked David to fill in and teach his class. David faked his way through it and finally ended up being an instructor for directing.

The woman David had come to New York with was now dating a television executive who had become the producer of the *Fred Waring Show*. She recommended David, and he was hired as assistant to the producer. This was his first professional job in television.

David went on to become the associate director of the Phil Silvers Show, *Bilko*, and directed several episodes. He then joined CBS television as a staff associate director. During vacations he would take free-lance jobs as a director for other shows. Eventually he left CBS and went out on his own as a free-lance director. David became very successful as a director for television shows.

When the 1970s rolled around, television was no longer in its golden years. The shows were now too formatted, and producers wanted to churn them out as fast as they could. The creativity and fun were gone. David turned sour on his profession. He didn't want to try directing for the movies. He wanted out.

In 1972, David said to himself, "How do I want to be remembered—in connection with tapes of old soaps? I really love to paint, and I think I can make a living at it."

David came home one day and had a conference with his wife and two teenage daughters. He told them what he wanted to do and asked what they thought of his plan. They were behind him 100 percent. He felt it would take a few years to be able to show in enough important galleries, so he wanted to take a second mortgage out on the house to see them through. David would have a cushion. No one would go hungry, and his two daughters could go to college.

The first exhibit, in November of 1972, was at St. Bart's in New York. David spent $3,000 in brochures, pamphlets and promotion pieces and announced the event to everyone he knew in the television business. The show consisted of 40 pieces in every medium—pencil, pastel, ink and large oil abstracts, and he sold very few. Next David made the rounds of all the galleries in Manhattan and got what he called, "a dreadful response." Only one gallery on Madison and 81st Street was interested. Later he found out that it was a *Vanity Gallery*. For $150 they would list an artist in their catalog and show at least one piece of art in the gallery. Amazingly enough, David did sell a few pieces. But he felt that now he had spent about $3,500 to learn what not to do.

What David did learn is that versatility is no virtue, that a *trademark* or *signature* of recognizability is essential. David had developed a unique, fluid style of painting abstracts, blending colors into each other and leaving large areas of white. He worked on large canvases and concentrated on creating his own signature.

Trying to break into New York was not going to work. David decided that his abstracts would have a better chance of selling in the Southeast and the Southwest. He had met numerous people during his years in television, and he decided to make an audio tape explaining that they all knew him as a director, a friend and an artist. He was now embarking on a campaign called D.A.R.E., David's Art Requires Exposure. The people he sent the tapes to were the kind who always threw cocktail parties. David's offer was to give them the opportunity to give their parties a theme using his art. He would bring in his paintings, hang them and light them. He offered the host $500 off on the painting of their choice. He urged them not to invite only friends and neighbors but also people who were interested in art. He got instant responses from several people around the country.

David loaded paintings in crates on top of his car, rented a trailer and drove to Florida. His first *in-home* exhibit was for two days in a friend's house in Key Biscayne. Then he did three more exhibits—one in Lighthouse Point, the other in Ft. Lauderdale and the last in Tampa. David was on the road constantly. He would hang and light the paintings, then visit every art gallery in each city. He would show the owners photographs of his work and tell them that his work was on exhibit in his friend's home and invite them to visit, have some coffee or a drink and view his work. David was able to secure quite a few galleries this way. Looking back, he said, "I can't believe my arrogance at offering $500 off on one of my paintings. I was assuming that they wanted one. What if they didn't even like my work? But in truth, I was very confident of my talent. To this day I am surprised at the enthusiastic response I received." That's how David got his paintings in galleries across the country.

In Houston, Texas, a public relations man bought several of David's paintings and started touting his talent. This brought David's work to the attention of the publisher of *Southwest Art* magazine, who came and visited one of David's in-home exhibits. The publisher was impressed with David's work and helped get him into a gallery in Houston, where he still exhibits today. The publisher also featured an article on David's work in a later edition of *Southwest Art*. Then the publisher told David that he wanted to purchase a painting for his office but didn't want to pay full price. David made him a proposition. He offered to let the publisher commission a painting that David would paint specifically for the office. They agreed on a price, but when David delivered the painting, he told the publisher to forget the money; he wanted to be on the front cover of *Southwest Art* magazine. The publisher's response was, "Geez, you don't want much, do you? I'm booked solid for my covers." David finally convinced him, and now he was armed with a cover and an article from a respected art magazine. This made him *legitimate*. It was David's breakthrough. He then had credentials when he called on new galleries.

David feels that his years of being in television gave him the business experience he needed and also the sense of showmanship necessary to do what he did in touring his paintings. He was not just going to sit around being turned down by galleries, or like many artists, set up his work on sidewalks in street fairs. He refused to cheapen his work that way.

"As a director, David said, "you learn arrogance. You're almost playing God every day. If you don't act like you are the best and know what you're doing, you get walked all over by the producer, the staff and the actors. You have to convince everyone on the set that your way is the only way. Otherwise you'd never get a show completed. And this arrogance works, so I used that same arrogance when I would walk into a gallery."

David also found that gallery owners were fascinated by his background as a director in television. He never realized that most people looked at his past as a glamorous one. He had never considered it such a big deal. But this almost always got him an audience with most gallery owners. He learned that this served him well, and he used it to the fullest.

A local TV station had read about David and wanted him as a guest on their morning show. David watched the show for several days to see what the format was. The day before he was to appear, he went to the studio and asked to see the host who would be interviewing him the next morning. David was told that the host was busy and also that such meetings were never done. The host would talk to him a few minutes before the show in the morning. That's the routine. David knew how TV worked, and he was damned if he would risk having his paintings hastily schlepped around on the wrong-sized easels and be at the mercy of poor, last-minute lighting. David wanted to see the studio and *direct* his appearance. David's arrogance won again. He refused to leave until the host became *unbusy*.

The next morning during the live show, the host kept looking at David's work on the set. It was obvious that the host had never seen David's work before. Just as the 20-minute segment was ending, the host blurted out, "Boy, you know I could really live with this stuff. This is *FANTASTIC.*" Then the segment faded to a commercial. After the show, David took advantage of the opportunity and negotiated to have the show's set decorated with his paintings, changing them on a regular basis and giving both David and the Houston gallery a credit at the end of each show. David had successfully used his years as a director to help promote himself and his work.

Another strategy David used was to take out full-page ads in art magazines. He would contact owners of galleries where he had paintings and tell them that he would list their galleries in his ad if they would contribute to the cost. He rarely paid for the ads himself, having convinced enough owners to participate.

David continued to use these tactics to gain exposure for his work. It took him seven years until he was selling enough paintings to consider himself comfortably supported by his painting and his career as an artist.

David did not make a plan before he started. He learned on the job. But he had determination, and he made an observation early that galleries are only stores that sell art. He looked for galleries that were selling paintings for slightly more than what he was asking. This association put him into the same arena as the other higher-priced artists. David shied away from *junk* galleries, knowing that he would end up being a cheap painter forever and never be taken seriously as an artist.

David had the full support of his family from the very beginning. They believed in him, and he believed in himself.

David works all day, every day except Sunday. His studio is the basement of his home in Leonia, New Jersey, where he lives with his wife, Bonnie. He makes his own frames, stretches the canvas, even makes his own shipping crates—although he admits to making them an inch too big or small sometimes and having to start over. David does all his own correspondence with galleries. His work day starts at 6:30 AM, and he works straight through until 6:00 PM. At the very beginning he realized that no one cares whether you get up early and work all day when you work for yourself. But if you want to be successful, you have to discipline yourself.

"Besides," he said, "I love what I'm doing. It's not really work." David has to force himself not to work on Sunday, but he knows he needs a day off to allow his mind to rest and let his subconscious mind work on new creations.

What is David's advice for others contemplating breaking the corporate bondage? "Don't do it the way I did. I didn't know what I was getting into. Had I known, I might not have tried it."

David recommends first deciding what you want to do. It should be something that is based on previous experience or something you're good at. Make a plan. Talk to people in the field you are considering, do a lot of research and make sure that you have a financial cushion so that anxiety doesn't interfere and disrupt your pursuit.

David's greatest benefit from making the break has not been the money. It's been the recognition, the satisfaction of knowing that people walk into a gallery and they buy David, "Me on canvas." David has made a lot of friends through his paintings. Many people who have purchased his paintings have written to him, and he corresponds with them on a regular basis. Many he has met personally, and they've become good friends.

David's works are displayed in many prominent galleries across the country. He gets commissioned to do paintings all the time. David has been painting full-time now for 20 years. He is 69, but you would never know it. He still works 12-hour days. He is full of vitality, contented and comfortable with himself. He will leave a legacy behind—David Grant Roth *will* be remembered.

Wilhelmina Michel-Weng: Photo by Michael Dainard

21

Urban Media

Wilhelmina Michel-Weng

Wilhelmina Michel-Weng is executive vice president and director of broadcast services for Urban Media, an advertising agency that bills in excess of $6 million a year. There's one big difference about this agency and her job there. Wilhelmina owns half of the agency.

Wilhelmina was born on January 15, 1952, in New York City. She attended grade school at Our Lady of Lourdes, and from the time she was six years old, her dream was to be a nurse. She attended Cathedral High School and still wanted to be a nurse, but after three years of volunteer nursing, she decided that this was not her calling in life. Next Wilhelmina attended Pace University and then New York School of Interior Design. She worked part-time for an interior design firm for three years while still attending school. She soon realized that this was also not the profession she wanted to pursue.

Wilhelmina's first real job was as a teletypist for New York Telephone. "The funny thing is," she said, "I couldn't type. I failed the typing test, but they attributed it to nervousness." Nine months later, she went to work as a receptionist at the Federal Reserve legal department. After a year, she still didn't quite know what she wanted to do. An article in a business publication caught her eye, and she decided that advertising might be the right career path.

Willie (as her friends call her) had a friend at the Wells, Rich, Greene Agency, but the friend refused to help her get an interview. Undaunted, Willie called personnel at Wells, Rich and got an interview. She was hired immediately as a receptionist in the creative area and then moved into the media department where she quickly discovered that this was something that intrigued her. "You didn't have to be a brain surgeon," Willie laughed. "This was something I could learn to do and probably like." She picked up quite a lot in a short period of time, and George Pine and Peter Doyle, from McGavren & Guild (radio sales representatives), asked her to join them as a receptionist and sales assistant.

After two years of radio experience, Willie joined WCBS TV as a sales assistant. "CBS was real corporate," she said, "I couldn't keep up with the politics. I probably could now, but then it was beyond me."

Willie met her future husband while at CBS, and even though they weren't in the same department and kept their relationship very quiet, she was asked to leave the company. She quickly landed a job at Allscope, a media buying agency where she really began to learn the media business.

Willie heard about a position at Marshall, Jordan Advertising for a media director and secured an interview. During the interview, she was asked for her resume.

"Well," she said, "my resume would have shown nothing but jobs as a receptionist and assistant, so I told them a piece of paper wasn't going to make any difference. This is me, ask me questions about the business and make a judgment. They hired me on the spot. It was tough because I was working until midnight most nights learning the business as I went. It took me 12 hours to do what would take me 5 hours now."

Willie learned the real guts of media in this position. She also learned the creative end, and most importantly, how to deal with people. "That's important," she said. "This is a real people business, and if you don't have people skills, you won't make it."

Willie left Marshall, Jordan to work at one of the top ten radio stations in New York as a sales executive. She did very well for almost five years until she was fired for rejecting what today would be termed *sexual harassment*. According to Willie, the company president tried to make a move on Willie at a Christmas party, and she refused his advances. Willie went on vacation, and after the holidays she returned to work. "I knew something was wrong right away." she said. "My sales manager called me into his office and told me he didn't know what was going on, but I was to be let go at once."

That afternoon she was given a memo stating that she was on probation for a month. No reason was given. The next morning Willie went to the general manager and told him, "This is a joke. After a month you're going to fire me. What's the reason?" The general manager couldn't answer her, and she told him she would make it easy for them. "Today will be my last day. Just give me a letter stating that I'm being let go for no reason, and I'll leave." It took him all day to compose a letter that praised her to no end, and that he would do anything to help her, but on the recommendation of her sales manager, she was being let go.

Willie took the letter and showed it to her sales manager. Two weeks later, he left, unable to deal with the situation. An associate gave her the name of an attorney, and she hired him. He took the case and never charged her. She had been the only woman on the sales staff and was being paid one-third what the men were. Although sexual harassment charges were not in fashion in the mid-1980s, the attorney used this as the charge. The radio station promptly made a satisfactory settlement, but Willie felt that a real injustice had been done to her. She turned sour on the corporate world.

Willie decided that she didn't ever want to work for a corporation again, and she toyed with the idea of opening a store. She stayed home for a year. Now that she was married, she and her husband tried unsuccessfully to have a baby. She felt she was too young to stay home, and besides she liked to stay active and enjoy accomplishments outside her home life. Willie actively pursued trying to open a retail business but realized she couldn't do it on her own. She wanted, and needed, a partner. At the time she was unsuccessful in finding one.

The president of a media company wanted Wilhelmina to work for him, but she was adamant about not returning to corporate life. He was persistent to the point of enlisting her husband to try to convince her. At last he persuaded her to work on one project for just three weeks, and Willie relented. After getting his grips on her, he then convinced her to stay two more weeks. He still tried to convince her to work full time. She refused.

Willie had to undergo surgery, and during her six-week convalescence, the president of the media company called her every day. Willie kept saying no and at the same time asking for perks that she knew he would refuse, hoping he would just go away. To her surprise he eventually met all her demands, and she returned to work in the corporate world.

It wasn't long before she realized what a bad decision she had made to work for this president. The only good thing that came from the association was that she met her future partner, Jay Levinson. They worked well together, and over the course of time, Jay started suggesting that they open their own media agency. Willie wasn't too keen on the idea at the time. Her dream was to own her own business, but she had always thought in terms of owning a store of some type. She was sure of two things, though: She wanted out of her present job, and she would never again allow herself to be talked into working for someone else.

According to Willie, her employer didn't like the fact that two of his employees were working so well together and tried to play each one against the other. Willie had had enough of this kind of corporate politics and decided that Jay's idea wasn't such a bad one. "What was the worst thing that could happen?" she asked herself. "I'll just be back where I started if it doesn't work." So Willie and Jay made the decision to open Urban Media and set a target date of six months to leave and open the new company. This was August 1987.

However, once the president found out about their plans, Willie and Jay knew that working there was no longer a feasible option. By the time that Willie packed her belongings at the office and left the company for good with Jay, she actually felt that she was escaping from corporate bondage.

That was Friday, November 13, 1987, and Willie and Jay had originally planned on leaving in January, 1988. They had made a deal with another firm that would give them office space, use of the conference rooms, reception-ist and other amenities. The problem was that this firm was in the process of moving to larger quarters, and everything was scheduled for a January move.

Fortunately the firm was able to accommodate them right away, and on Monday, November 16, 1987, Urban Media opened its doors for business. The partners had very little money, and it took five months before they had any money coming in. It wasn't easy, but they were both determined. Willie felt that she had been *molested* by the corporate world twice. It would never happen again— ever. Willie had the motivation, and she had all the right stuff to make it work.

Today Urban Media is a well-respected company that places media for many well-known names. They bill more than $6 million a year, and business continues to expand.

It was never Wilhelmina's *dream* to own a media company. When pressed for an answer to what her *dream* is, it's hard for her to answer. In reflection, she feels she is extremely happy today. The business is something she really enjoys doing. She and her partner call all the shots. "It's a dream that has made itself evolve and come true," she said. "It has its ups and downs, but I love it. Not a day goes by that I don't think how lucky I am."

Willie's advice to others contemplating making a move is, "Take a chance.What's the worst possible thing that could happen if you fail? You just go back to square one and start over. You can always go back and get a job if you need to. If you're willing to work hard and believe in yourself, you'll be successful."

Another of Willie's dreams is coming true. She and her husband, Laurie, are expecting their first child in May of 1993. It's taken nine years of specialists and tests, but Willie doesn't give up on anything. When she sets her mind to something, you can bet on her making it happen. The best thing about her pregnancy is that she doesn't have to worry about how much time she can take for maternity leave and *at-home time* with her new baby. It's her call.

Bill Young: Photo by Michael Dainard

Global English

Bill Young

Ask Bill Young about his new company, Language Performance, and get ready for a real education about what the changes in Central Europe and Russia mean to the world of business. One of the most innovative aspects of Bill's new business is Global English. "Global English," he says, "is more than English—it's an attitude."

With the end of the Cold War, Central Europe and Russia are ushering in an unprecedented international business climate—new markets, experimental business models, socialist economics in transition, changing consumer needs, a new managerial and executive class and redistribution of political power.

These developments signal the movement of money away from national economics toward global, interdependent economic webs. The strength of these webs depends upon cooperation among people who speak different languages. Corporations from all the major business centers of the world will be working with new partners from Central Europe and Russia. A common spoken language will be shared by all of these people: English.

Bill Young has built an exciting new company based on this premise, and he's already lined up his first customers in Czechoslovakia. Quite a number of companies teach ESL, English as a Second Language, but not the way Bill is doing it. His method will include what he calls PCS, Personal Culture Services. This new element differentiates him from the competition. Bill's market research shows there are more than 400 million potential customers in Central Europe and Russia for his new services. If Bill Young is right, he should be busy for a very long time.

Forty-nine-year-old Bill Young was born in Fresno, California. His first childhood memory was the piano. Bill's mother was an extraordinary pianist, and Bill was playing the piano at three years old. He attended the public schools in Fresno but was not a very good student. "I had a difficult time motivating myself," he said, "I loved music and politics—student politics. I also liked literature, history and art." Fresno was a big church city in the 1950s, and Bill was a member of the choir. He also did some preaching as a child. "That's how I learned my acting skills," he said, "by standing up in front of a congregation and preaching the gospel every Sunday."

Bill had a very good voice, and in high school he acted in the theater groups—mostly musicals. His first role was Curly in *Oklahoma*. He also sang in statewide choir competitions. His brother was a jazz drummer, and Bill took an interest in jazz. He wrote his first song at age 15. His first real job after graduation was in forestry. He loved the outdoors and was seriously considering becoming a forest ranger.

Bill attended Fresno State College. His main interests were in communications, music, theater and the arts, but his father was against it. "My father flat out told me that if I wanted to study music and the arts," Bill said, "he wouldn't pay for college. My mother agreed even though she had a career as a pianist. They liked my playing well enough, but they wanted me to become a respectable businessman and earn a good living." Bill's first major was in history, and he studied speech pathology and psychology. Bill had the same girlfriend since the age of 13. Their plan after college was to open a speech and hearing clinic in Fresno.

In 1963 Bill's father died, and his mother just sort of *checked out* for a while. Bill's brother went bankrupt. Next, his girlfriend of seven years broke up with him. Bill was devastated and started to have problems in school.

"I was a mess, " he said. "I quit going to classes. I started drinking a lot. I had this sports car and would drive around in the middle of winter with the top down. I ended up with pneumonia. It was just crazy stuff. The draft was heating up with Vietnam, so I joined the Army."

After he was discharged from service, Bill and a friend traveled around Europe for a year. He realized that music was what he really wanted and returned to Fresno State college to earn a degree in music and theater. In 1966, Bill went to San Francisco State University to earn his masters degree in music composition. During this time, he composed a lot of music. He started working on a PhD and thought he would pursue a career in academia, teaching music and composition. For three years, he was an associate professor. During this time he got married. In his spare moments he wrote music for the theater.

Politics had always been another of Bill's interests. He felt very strongly about the war in Vietnam. "It was a very complex situation," he said, "trying to teach music composition to a group of students who were constantly terrified of being drafted."

The Bay area was experiencing a lot of domestic unrest at that time. Bill felt that the university president—a retired Navy Commander—had absolutely no interest in education. Bill became disenchanted with teaching, and the writing wasn't earning him much money. He and his wife wanted to travel, so he quit the university and used the money from his retirement fund to move to Ireland. After nine months, his wife decided to go to Israel, and Bill traveled around North Africa on his own for a while. When his money ran out, he returned to San Francisco and opened up a voice studio and a theater group. He coached singers and actors, wrote music and did a lot of acting.

Bill's reputation as a voice teacher grew steadily, and he started doing a lot of consulting work for foundations. He also taught part-time at several universities. He and his second wife founded the San Francisco School of Dramatic Arts. He started voice consulting for businesses, including working with trial lawyers who wanted to improve their courtroom dramatics. Bill realized that his background in theater and speech was extraordinarily useful in the world of business.

The economic situation became a disaster, and since a lot of Bill's income came from foundations and publicly funded nonprofit groups, he felt the pinch. During this period, Bill divorced his second wife. By 1982, his theater group went bust, and he started trying to figure out what to do next. Bill turned to the world of business and started doing a lot of consulting with the media coaching and training newscasters.

Bill married for the third time. His wife is a graphic designer and writer who does a lot of public speaking. She was initially a client of Bill's—sent to him for speech coaching to get rid of her French accent. Bill had a strict policy of not getting involved with any clients. He couldn't help himself, and he's glad he made an exception. His wife had done a lot of design work for magazines, and in 1989 Condé Nast asked her to come to New York to redesign *Self Magazine*.

Bill was not happy with things in San Francisco at the time, and he really loved New York. With very little hesitation, he broke his corporate bondage and left a successful 20-year career in San Francisco to move to New York. He arrived with nothing more than his music and a handful of recommendations from companies, schools and foundations he had worked with in the past.

Bill got a job for two years at NYU with the music theater program, then a teaching job at the Lincoln Center Institute. He was back in the world of academia. He managed to build up a small number of students for speech training, did voice-over work for documentaries, voice-over for commercials and a variety of consulting jobs. Bill was busy doing a lot of things to earn a living. Even though he was basically working for himself, there was no direction or plan to what he was doing. He had worked himself into a shiny new set of corporate chains, depending upon his teaching posts and all of these other activities to earn his living.

Bill had never considered himself to be an innovative business person. He had a lot of talent, skill and education, but they were not being directed or focused into a real business. His dream was to be able to do something that would combine all of his talents and the things he liked to do. In 1991 he interviewed a career consultant who tried to help him put his scattered activities together, but it didn't work, and he became more frustrated with where his life was going. Bill began to panic and became gripped with fear that he didn't have a real job. He had a lot of things going for him, and he was making money. He seemed to be bouncing all over the place.

Bill had a tremendous amount of energy and a lot of different interests. The basic problem was that there was no one thing that he could say he wanted to devote himself to. If he did, he was afraid he would become bored. He needed to combine as many of the various talents and skills as possible and make them into a career. He knew he could always find work in the corporate world and could always make money—that wasn't the problem. Bill wanted to be happy. One of his major problems was that he didn't want to just own a business. He thought it would be too boring. He needed a challenge, something that would make him feel that he was making a contribution.

In 1991 Bill was invited to be a committee chairman at an environmental conference in Czechoslovakia. One of the biggest problems at the conference involved the language barriers that existed among the committee delegates from many different countries. English and Slovak were the basic languages of the conference, and even though there were translators, they were generally from the host's country. These translators didn't understand the cultural differences and nuances. It seemed to Bill that this caused a lot of misunderstanding among members. That's when he first got the germ of an idea for a new company.

From January through March of 1992, Bill was hired to work with a theatrical production company on a play called *Metro* in Warsaw, Poland. He worked with the 38-member cast of the play—only seven knew English. Bill worked 16-hour days and became very close to the play's cast and crew. The seven who knew English had never been to America; the translators for the rest hadn't either. Bill found that this caused a tremendous amount of confusion sometimes in understanding his direction. ESL was not sufficient. Many English words have double, sometimes triple meanings. Also, not knowing the customs or culture caused even more misinterpretation.

Bill returned to New York with an idea of what was needed if he were to continue working in European countries. He realized that there was also an opportunity for developing a consulting service to others. What Bill didn't have was a plan of how to put it together. He took a crash course in *How To Market Yourself* and developed a personal marketing plan.

In July of 1992, Bill opened his new company, Global English. His new venture combines many of his skills and talents, and best of all, most of the things he likes to do. He loves to travel and has toured Europe extensively. He also loves to teach and has an expansive knowledge of Socialism and Marxism. His background in speech, acting, music and drama, ties it all together. Bill's greatest reward is that he now knows exactly what he wants, and he is doing it. His corporate chains, some of his own making, are gone forever.

Global English doesn't just teach English; it adds Personal Culture Services (PCS), which form the framework for studying the psychology and cultural background of one's potential business associate. With this kind of information, an executive can be sensitive to his or her future business partner, bringing comfort and reassurance to the atmosphere of any negotiation. For example, familiarity with the following subjects would provide a secure setting for productive interaction: political attitudes, social mannerisms, sexual politics, art, music, literature, food, contemporary events, clothing style and grooming.

Bill uses a fictional scenario to illustrate the need for Personal Culture Services. The players are: Wagner & Reumfeld, a large American corporation with a division that deals exclusively with leather products; Krywosz, a Polish company specializing in bookstores, publishing, shoe manufacturing and leather distribution; Mrs. Margaret Courtney, Division President of Barbara Stamford, a major United States retailer of leather handbags.

The scenario: In April of 1989, Wagner & Reumfeld purchased Krywosz for $4.5 million. The condition of the sale included a major upgrading of the leather supply and marketing/distribution side of Krywosz. The previous owner and president of the Polish company, Wiktor Janowski, was to remain on salary and continue his role as company president. Mr. Janowski is in his early 40s, educated in economics, has a efficient grasp of English and knows Poland's domestic economy—including the potential business hazards involved in running a corporation in an economy going through *shock therapy.*

On February 19, 1991, at 8:22 AM, Wagner & Reumfeld received a phone call from Margaret Courtney. The purpose of her call was to inform Wagner & Reumfeld that she was trying to locate fine, premium-quality hides to manufacture a new line of handbags for the Barbara Stamford company.

Wagner & Reumfeld suggested that she call Krywosz directly in Warsaw. Mrs. Courtney called Krywosz and was informed that Mr. Janowski was not in but would return the call when he arrived.

After two hours, she tried again and was informed that Mr. Janowski was in an urgent meeting but would return her call as soon as possible. Mrs. Courtney faxed a detailed letter of what she needed, hoping to speed things up.

The next morning, Mrs. Courtney discovered that there was no return fax or phone call. She called again. The receptionist knew who she was by this time and put her right through to Mr. Janowski. When he answered, he said, "Mr..., excuse me, what is your name?" Perturbed from the beginning, Mrs. Courtney repeated her name and company, then proceeded to explain her needs for quality hides.

During the course of the conversation, Mrs. Courtney had difficulty understanding Janowski's strongly accented English. Also his phone manner was aggressive. She constantly asked for clarification of things he said, and he became impatient with her. Then Mr. Janowski became more than a little casual with her.

Mrs. Courtney realized that she was more caught up and distracted by Mr. Janowski's manner than she was in the business at hand. When Mrs. Courtney concluded the phone call, she felt very annoyed and insecure about dealing with Krywosz. She placed an order with another firm in Hong Kong. Wagner & Reumfeld lost out on a $2 million deal.

Bill's analysis of the scenario is that Wagner & Reumfeld should have made the initial contact with their Polish company on Mrs. Courtney's behalf. They should have been aware that in many countries, men are the *chiefs*, and are generally aggressive, impatient and familiar when dealing with women in the workplace. Also, strong regional accents often contribute to misunderstandings. The cultural aspect of Mr. Janowski's attitude lost the deal.

Bill's new company, if hired by Wagner & Reumfeld, would have prevented that. His coaching of both the American side and the Polish side would have made the difference in how business should be conducted between companies of different languages and, more importantly, cultures.

Bill Young should do well with his new company. There is certainly a need for his services as we become more global, and the barriers of Eastern European countries continue to disappear. Bill is not as caught up with *doing well* as he is about finally recognizing his dream and pursuing it.

Sources for Additional Reading

The Complete Guide to Consulting Success,
Howard Shenson and Ted Nicholas
Enterprise • Dearborn, 1993

Don't Shoot Yourself in the Left Foot: A Workbook for Success
Dr. Daniel Amen
Warner Books, 1992

How To Market Yourself
Michael Dainard
Union Square Press, 1990

How To Buy a Business
Richard Joseph, Anna Nekoranec and Carl Steffens
Enterprise • Dearborn, 1992

The 100 Best Jobs for the 1990s and Beyond
Carol Kleiman
Dearborn Financial Publishing, Inc., 1992

Making the Most of Your Money: A Comprehensive Guide to Financial Planning, 1991
Jane Bryant Quinn
Simon & Schuster, 1991

The Small Business Bible: Make-or-Break Factors for Survival and Success
Paul Resnick
John Wiley & Sons, 1988

The Executive Success Diet
June Roth, M.S. & Harvey M. Ross, M.D.
McGraw-Hill, 1986

Terry Savage Talks Money: The Common-Sense Guide to Money Matters
Terry Savage
Dearborn Financial Publishing, Inc., 1990

The Growth Challenge: How To Build Your Business Profitably
Stephen A. Stumpf
Enterprise • Dearborn, 1993

Do What You Love, The Money Will Follow: Discovering Your Right Livelihood
Marsha Sinetar
Dell Trade Paperback, 1989

High Finance on a Low Budget
Mark and Jo Ann Skousen
Dearborn Financial Publishing, Inc., 1993

Scrooge Investing: The Bargain Hunter's Guide to Discounts, Free Services, Special Privileges and 99 Other Money-Saving Tips
Mark Skousen
Dearborn Financial Publishing, Inc., 1992

Index